A Doc's Testimony

FROM INJURY TO IRONMAN

Larry D. Perry III

As told to Dr. Cristy Kessler

For information about Larry D. Perry III, media interviews, or to book Larry for your next event, please visit www.larryperryiii.com

Book Layout ©2017 BookDesignTemplates.com

Ordering Information:
Quantity sales. Special discounts are available on quantity purchases by corporations, associations, and others. For details, contact us at www.larryperryiii.com

A Doc's Testimony: From Injury to Ironman by Larry D. Perry III—1st ed.
ISBN 978-0-9899987-5-8

Contents

Dedication

To Jenn, my dearest wife, thank you for the love and support you've given me through this process. I truly love you with all of my mind, heart and soul.

Madison and Ava, Daddy loves you so much and I hope this book will help you to see everything I've been through and how much I love you. I also hope you will see the faith and dedication that I devote to being your father, and being the best dad I can be for you guys.

Levi, my little miracle boy, I love you so much and I want you to know how blessed I am to have you in my life. May you also see the faith and dedication I have to being the best dad I can be to you.

Donald Steven "Joker" Brown, you are missed tremendously by your family and peers. I think about you often. The smile you wore on your face all the time and your love for Jesus is something that I miss about you regularly. To the Brown family, I am sorry for the loss of your son, brother, nephew, and grandson, but know for sure that he is watching over us all.

Charles "Chuck" Komppa, I know we just met that fateful day of your death, but I appreciate you stepping in to drive our HMMWV back to our Base. Your selfless service to our platoon that day and to this country is something that none of us will ever forget. To the Komppa family, I am so sorry for your loss and I know that heaven gained a great man the day Chuck went to be with the Lord.

God Bless and thank you everyone for supporting me.

Lord, As I embark upon this path that you, in your infinite wisdom, have set before me, I pray that you will guide my hand, my heart and my mind. Keep me faithful to my oath, always aware of the seriousness of my duties, and above all the sacredness of life. Let me not be a glory seeker, but rather a servant, as You the Great Physician to whom all Glory belongs, served even us. Help me face the trials before me, death of those I come to love, and personal disappointments without losing heart or faith. May I place first the welfare of those entrusted to my care, and self-last. Above all Lord, protect me from my pride, for there is nothing I can do through what skill I may possess that is not in your will that it be done. Amen.

—JRT, veteransprayers2.tripod.com

Foreword

There is no reason why my path in life should have crossed Larry Perry's path. We have never shared the same geography. I grew up in Southern California and spent the majority of my adult life moving every few years as a member of the Air Force. Larry was raised in Maryland and called wherever the Navy took him, "home". While the connection we both have is military service, we are pursuing very different careers outside of the military. There is no reason why our paths should have crossed, but I am glad they did.

Larry and I were brought together through a military veteran mentorship program called American Corporate Partners (www.acp-usa.org). Through a formal matching process, we agreed to commit to a year-long mentorship program. I was looking to assist a fellow veteran in making a smooth transition into corporate America after going through the transition myself. Larry was looking for a way to put the numerous ideas he had into action. We quickly realized that our relationship was not going to follow the typical path of career guidance, interview preparation, and resume feedback. Larry had a different set of ideas, and I was there to coach him along. When we first talked, Larry was an untapped spring ready to burst. When Larry did bring his ideas to the surface, our purpose together became clear.

Larry and I were brought together not by accident, but by the grace of God. Larry was the sole survivor of an improvised explosive device (IED) attack while deployed to Operation IRAQI FREEDOM in October of 2006. His road to recovery and his survivorship would be the reason we were brought together. We were connected almost to the exact one-year anniversary of my wife being diagnosed with metastatic cancer. While Larry and I were laying out a plan for our mentor-protégé relationship, my wife, Lisa, and I were struggling to understand how our lives changed and what we could expect in the future. By the grace of God, Larry and I were connected to help each other live for today, while making our dreams a reality.

Larry and I shared a monthly phone call during our mentor relationship. We always started the call by catching up on family. He let me into my inner circle and shared with me the difficulty he and

his wife were having conceiving a child. He shared with me his hopes and fears when his wife did become pregnant. But true to Larry's spirit as a survivor, he did not focus on the odds. Rather, Larry put his trust in God to carve his path in life as a husband and father. It was always a relief to hear from Larry every month that Jenn's pregnancy was progressing to full term. Larry's steadfast faith bore fruit on January 14, 2017 when Jenn gave birth to little Levi Perry.

Steve and me at Fells Point in Baltimore, August 2017.

As a survivor, Larry has the sense of purpose of someone who knows that tomorrow is not a given. He knows that we see our next "tomorrow" only by the grace of God. When we connected month-after-month, Larry showed up with a new challenge each time. He moved with a sense of purpose and without regard for the odds he faced. That is not to say that Larry was reckless. Far from that, Larry is free. Larry is free to pursue the impossible because he knows we live through God's grace. He also carries on the spirit of those who made the ultimate sacrifice on the day Larry now refers to as "Alive Day". Larry is free to live, free to forgive, free to love, and free to dream.

I leave you to enjoy Larry's story with an update from my family's journey. During a visit to the University of Kansas Cancer Center, Lisa's oncologist looked at both of us and said, "The best revenge you can have on cancer is to live a good life. Go live."

Lt Col Steven R. Marin, USAF (Ret)

Prologue

"Doc Perry's Alive! Doc Perry's Alive!" These are the words Corporal James Steuter was screaming as he ran around my Humvee after it had been hit. It was October 25, 2006.

I didn't hear a boom. I don't remember anything until I woke up about 9 hours later. What I'm telling you now is what I've been told. I was blown thirty-five feet out of the vehicle and off to the right. I wasn't wearing my seat belt and that's why I lived. The driver of my truck was blown to pieces. They found his spine had been ripped out and the rest of his body was in chunks. The gunner was nearly decapitated from the blast injury that blew the turret off the vehicle.

Corporal Steuter came running to me and he saw that my arm was all messed up and my leg was in shambles. My face and legs were covered in blood from shrapnel wounds. The blast tore through my meniscus and the ligaments inside my knee, particularly the ACL and MCL. Because the meniscus, ACL, and MCL were torn, my foot was turned around so my toes were pointed to the ground instead of into the air. The blast tore up my left knee and punctured a hole through my left leg. My right knee had a tear down the outside from being hit on something as I was blown out of the vehicle. Since we took the blast on the driver's side and I was sitting on the passenger's side, the radio in the middle broke free and smashed into my left elbow, causing it to be shattered into hundreds of pieces. My shattered elbow caused my arm to dangle and barely hang on. My left tricep was damaged as well. With my left elbow smashed and the tricep torn up, my arm was totally dismantled. The only thing that would keep my arm and left leg intact would be external fixators that would be attached later when I was in one of two surgical centers in Iraq.

Corporal Steuter saw so much blood, he realized my injuries were much worse than anticipated. After calling for help from Staff Sergeant Marcus Wilson, they both ran over to me to try and stop the bleeding. Marcus was cutting my pant leg off and he said he was in such a hurry to cut it off that he stabbed me by accident. According to him I screamed, "You M*****F***er! You stabbed me!" He said, "Doc, you've got far worse injuries than this stab wound I just gave you."

Article by the Cecil Whig about my Purple Heart. On display were some of the military coins I received from some of the Generals and other high ranking officials who came to see me.

These two guys needed to put a tourniquet on my leg and a tourniquet on my arm. I needed to be prepped for the mobile assault to come and get me and take me to the Landing Zone (LZ) for the helicopter. They needed to get me out of there fast; I was losing a lot of blood. But this would be no easy extraction.

While they were working on me, we started taking fire from people hiding out in the palm groves and those palm trees by the bridge. The actual IED blast had blown off my Kevlar helmet. My flak jacket, which was 20/30 pounds with Small Arms Protective Insert (SAPI) plates and all my gear attached, had been ripped off by the blast. Here I was, losing blood and unable to move, without any protection. So Steuter had to lay head to head with me and Marcus laid the other way where his feet were at my head on the back side of me. They were shielding me so I wouldn't get shot. Both men, at this point, weren't even sure they would be able to get me to the LZ alive.

CHAPTER 1

The Explosion

"I knew, without a doubt, the Holy Spirit was talking to me and telling me not to wear a seat belt."

On October 25, 2006, in Haditha, Iraq, in the Al Anbar province, I woke up like any other normal day as a corpsman. Today, my platoon was going on a mission. A company in the Marine Corps consists of four platoons. I was stationed with Echo Company, 2nd Battalion 3rd Marines (2/3), in the 4th platoon, which was the Mobile Assault Platoon (MAP). The other three platoons were all foot patrols, so they would leave the base and walk the streets looking for bad guys. In the Mobile Assault Platoon, we were on Mission Squad one day and Quick Reaction Force (QRF) the next day. QRF is like being on call: we wait for the foot patrol platoons to call us and say that they were involved in a fire fight and we would go out and supply heavier fire for them when they were being pinned down by fire. If someone got shot or injured out there, the QRF would respond to retrieve the injured Marine and get them back to base to be treated or get them to the Landing Zone (LZ) to be transported by helicopter to a different base, like Al Asad or Balad, for surgery.

Today would be a typical mission for us. We traveled by convoy to deliver goods and/or we traveled to headquarters. Headquarters was located near Haditha Dam in Haditha, Iraq. On this day, like so many others, we were heading up to headquarters at Haditha Dam. We left our base around 9 am. Our job today was to transport a prisoner we had caught, a sniper who had killed one of our lieutenants, to headquarters. He shot the lieutenant between the eyes. We had the prisoner in one vehicle and the lieutenant's belongings in another vehicle so his belongings could be shipped back to his family. These were the everyday reminders that life could be taken away in a flash.

We arrived at headquarters and we had about four hours of free time before heading back. I always looked forward to being around the other corpsmen. Today was no different. We all congregated in the radio room to be ready to act in an instant if any of our guys came under fire. While all of us were catching up on the latest news from back home, it came across the radio that one of our Marines had died in combat. What should be such a tragic bit of news now found all of us somewhat unfazed, meaning that losing our comrades was more the norm than it ever should have been. And the day moved on from there. I left the communications room and took a nice long, hot shower. Our base only had cold water so I always enjoyed the opportunity to take a shower and put on a pair of clean socks. It sounds weird talking about socks but it is an important part of military combat life. You must make sure that you keep your feet in good condition and do all you can to avoid blisters and athlete's foot.

Before I realized it, four hours had passed and it was time to prepare for our convoy to return to our camp. I had been reflecting on the events that had occurred in my convoy. Our platoon hadn't been hit by an IED yet. However, we were in a convoy with another company, not attached to 2/3, who had three vehicles. Together we had one 7-ton and five HMMWV's with us. I was in Truck 2 during this convoy. My spotter, Steuter, noticed a piece of trash laying in the road that was not there before and he thought that maybe there was a pressure plate IED below. Steuter was one of the best spotters we had and, sure enough, there was an IED. He told all of us to stay to the right of this piece of trash. The other group, a Civilian Affairs company with the three additional convoy vehicles who were with us, did not have any PRRs (a headset able to communicate between 30 to 100 meters), a communication device we wore on our ears to communicate between trucks. They did not know to move to the right. In a split second, their first truck hit the IED. It was nighttime and it was a huge, massive fireball explosion. The enemy was using acetylene tanks to rig up their IEDs. The IEDs were made up of shells filled with rocks, nails, and everything else they could pack into the shells. I was in the second truck that day when I saw and heard the fireball. They had two corpsmen in three trucks so I had to run all the way back from my truck to the explosion and tend to the driver. There is no time to waste when part of your team is involved in an IED explosion. The driver had a hole through his right leg that broke his tibia and fibula. A motor mount came through the bottom of the truck and just kept going straight through his leg. I had to run a long way, and this was a major eye-opener for me. It was at this point and time, I decided not to wear my seat belt anymore on missions. I didn't have the time to deal with a seat belt system designed to keep me in the truck when I needed to high-tail it to those who are injured. That night, just two days before my Humvee would be hit by an IED, I prayed to God to protect me and give me guidance in my job as a corpsman. I felt completely calm in my decision to no longer wear my seat belt.

Back to the day of my accident. It was between 1:30 and 2:30 in the afternoon, and we were bringing back with us some additional vehicles along with some Navy reservists, one who was a hull tech and one who was an electrician, assigned to repair things at our camp. Because of the additional vehicles, we needed to switch drivers around. My normal driver was reassigned to drive the 7-ton behind me because he was from the motor pool and he had his 7-ton license. The guy who drove my truck was a Navy reservist from Montana, Chuck Komppa, and he volunteered to drive the truck. The reason we went on the mission was to bring back other vehicles. We needed a new 7-ton, and we also needed to bring the Navy guys down to fix some of our plumbing, water issues and electrical issues. We needed better hot water and we were having draining issues in our showers and washers.

We started driving back and there was the bridge that had been blown out a few weeks ago. Because of an IED blast taken by the other Mobile Assault Platoon a few weeks prior, it was decided every time we went through this bridge area we would always go around to the one side opposite of where the IED was hit before. When we were going up, we always went to the left and when we were coming back, we always went right.

As we approached the bridge, I was on my PRR asking the truck in front of me if we were okay to stay in their tracks. Sgt. Tarr, who was our Platoon Leader, said, "Yeah. We don't see anything. You're good. Stay in our tracks." So my driver stayed in their tracks. We needed to hold a nice, steady pace. Chuck held a steady pace as best he could, but I knew sitting next to him how nervous he was to be driving around that bridge. Chuck wasn't with us when the first IED explosion took place at the bridge, so he was paying extra close attention to keep us in the tracks of the truck in front of us. To the left of the bridge, somebody was hiding in the palm groves, a bunch of palm trees planted between the road and Euphrates River. And that somebody was holding a grill switch igniter that was connected to a copper wire that went down to a buried IED. Without a second thought, that somebody hit the ignitor and blew us up.

My truck was hit and there were three of us inside: my driver, Charles "Chuck" Komppa; my guy up in the turret who was in the gun that spun around on the top of the truck, Donald Brown; and me. I was in the passenger seat and I mentioned before that I had decided not to wear my seat belt anymore. My platoon commander at the time, who was our Staff Sergeant because our Lieutenant had gone to another platoon, was on the radio saying, "Everybody make sure you wear seat belts," among other things. But I was the only corpsman in 13 vehicles, and there was no way that I was going to wear my seat belt. If something happened in the back, I had to get out as fast as I could. Our seat belts were three-point harnesses. One strap came over each shoulder and then buckled down around your stomach area, and a buckle that came up through your legs. It was almost like a child's car seat. Once I could get out of the seat belt, there's a good half a mile to a mile to run with gear. I would either have to take my big medic sack with all my medical equipment or grab my little one and run back. I knew, without a doubt, the Holy Spirit was talking to me and telling me not to wear a seat belt.

We hit the IED on the driver's side. Everything that was in the center of the truck, the radio and Blue Force Tracker GPS that was located in front of me and to the left hanging off the dash, hit me and forced me out of the vehicle. I went flying. My platoon commander, Staff Sgt. Wilson, who was in the 7-ton behind me with the driver usually in my truck, said I was blown approximately 35 feet from my vehicle. The explosion stopped our convoy in its tracks and our spotter, Corporal James Steuter, started running around looking for survivors. He saw me raise my hand up in the air. He came running over to me and got on the radio yelling, "Doc Perry's alive, Doc Perry's alive." That is when he and Staff Sgt. Wilson saved my life.

Chapter 2

Leaving Iraq

"Mom?" and then the phone cut out. I called back again, "Mom, I'm hurt." And the phone cut out again. I yelled to the docs in the tent, "Move me closer to the edge. I need to call my mom NOW!"

I don't know how long the three of us laid there among the palm trees trying to stay protected from the gun fire. It could have been 30 seconds, it could have been hours. When you are under attack like this, no matter how much experience you have, your adrenaline is pumping and time has no significance. You just want to stay alive. Thank God Steuter and Marcus were there. They were my lifeline.

The other platoon finally got to us and put me in the back of a high back with steel gates up the back of the Humvee. The purpose of the high back is to transport people safely from place to place. I don't remember anything on our way to the Landing Zone so I could be transported by helicopter to a field hospital. I don't recall talking, I don't remember being conscious. I don't remember any of it. Shock had set in. My other corpsman, Carlos Soto, who was in the same platoon as I was, told me later that he kept me talking the whole time. He asked me about my motorcycle and how fast I had gone on it. He said he just kept me talking the whole time. Supposedly I told him I had gone as fast as hundred and sixty-five miles an hour. (Really, though, I've been about 175 mph so I told him that later when he called me from a satellite phone to talk to me while I was in the hospital.)

The helicopter took me to Al-Asad, which was one of the bigger bases in Iraq. They had a surgical unit there. It wasn't the main surgical unit in Iraq but it was located at a bigger base. Upon arrival, I went through some sort of procedure. The docs opened my stomach, removed my spleen since it had been ruptured in the explosion, and stabilized me for transport to Balad.

Balad is the bigger surgical unit that was in Iraq and it was there that I woke up. Nine hours had passed since the explosion and it was about 11:00 pm. I woke up and I looked down at my body. My left arm had an external fixator and so did my left leg. "What happened?!?!" And this is when I was told that I was blown up by an IED. "Where are my guys?!?!" And that's when they told me that I was the sole survivor. My only response was, "I need a phone. I need to call my mom NOW." I took the satellite phone and dialed my parents' house. "Mom?" and then the phone cut out. I called back again, "Mom, I'm hurt." And the phone cut out again. By this point my mom was flipping out. She had started calling the Red Cross and any number she had to try and figure out what had happened to me. I yelled to the docs in the tent, "Move me closer to the edge. I need to call my mom NOW!" I was lying in the dead center of the tent on a makeshift gurney and this made satellite reception very difficult. The gurney was a stretcher that was set atop two metal legs, like a saw horse used in construction, that held the litter (stretcher). It took a good 10 or 15 minutes before I could get a couple of guys to move me to the edge of the tent. Finally, I had a strong signal and I called mom again, "Mom, I've been hurt. I am alive. I am still in Iraq in a field hospital and they are preparing to send me to Germany for medical care."

CHAPTER 3

Coming Home

"In all of my haziness, I said to myself, right then and there, I WILL walk and I'm going to walk out of this hospital before I go back to the States."

I was flown from Balad, Iraq, to Landstuhl, Germany, by medivac, which is about a six hour flight. Due to the nature of my injuries and the heavy pain medications, I don't remember an awful lot about Germany. What I do remember is that I had a feeding tube, lots of IV bags hanging everywhere, and doctors and nurses coming in and out all the time checking on me. I was thirsty – dried-out, desert, cotton-mouth thirsty. But I couldn't drink anything because of the feeding tube. I am not sure of the doses or amounts of medications that were given to me, but regardless, I blatantly remember the doctor saying, "You may never walk again." In all of my haziness, I said to myself, right then and there, "I WILL walk and I'm going to walk out of this hospital before I go back to the States." I was in the hospital in Germany from October 26, 2006 until October 30, 2006.

On October 30th, between 11:15 and 11:30 at night, I arrived in the states via medical transport to the National Naval Medical Center in Bethesda, Maryland. I flew from Landstuhl to Andrews Air Force

Base in Maryland, about a 7 to 8 hour flight. Yes, I do remember the flight from Germany. Walking out of the hospital in Germany wasn't possible and after learning how extensive my injuries were, I wasn't surprised or disappointed. I still had made the promise to myself that I would walk again. It would just take a little longer. So I was loaded onto a C130, lying on a stretcher. We injured armed service

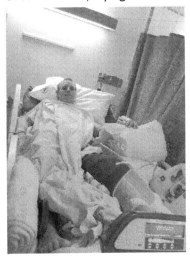

personnel were stacked two deep, like bunk beds, the entire length of the plane. I was on the top bunk. The nursing team removed the feeding tube before I was transported to the airstrip. I could eat and drink. And I remember eating about 10 packs of Graham crackers because all they had on the plane were Graham crackers and apple juice. I drank three or four of those round little containers of apple juice. It tasted like a gourmet meal after not having eaten real

At NNMC Bethesda.

food since before my accident. "Hey, can I get some more crackers and can I get another juice?" And the flight crew told me, "You need to be careful because eventually you will need to use the bathroom and you can't get down from there."

Being sent to Bethesda for my long-term medical care was an amazing blessing for me because I am from Maryland. Once we landed at Andrews Air Force Base and were transported by bus to the hospital, it was Halloween 2006. I asked if I could use a cell phone to call my mom to let her know I was state-side. I don't remember if my parents came down the next day or the day after. My first 24 hours at Bethesda were a parade of doctors coming in and out, doing assessments and deciding on a treatment plan. Most importantly, my medical team was deciding what surgery to do first, second, third, and so forth. There would be so many surgeries during my recovery process.

Surgeries began the next day and they would be every Monday and Friday until the day before Thanksgiving 2006. The surgeries were done to clean out my arm where the elbow was crushed and to clean my leg from the puncture hole at the knee. The day before Thanksgiving, the doctors were ready to proceed with skin grafts to close the open wounds on my leg and elbow. That surgery was seven hours long and quite extensive. In the recovery room, post-surgery, I had a fever that I just couldn't break. I was so cold, I was shivering, and my temperature fluctuated between 103 and 105. At one point, it reached 106 and it just wouldn't break for a long time.

While I was in the hospital at Bethesda, I ran into a corpsman, Jeff. I had worked with Jeff at MCRD San Diego and he was in Haditha with a Scout Sniper Platoon of Marines. Our paths crossed in Iraq when he came through our base at some point. And now he was here at Bethesda, and I wanted to see him.

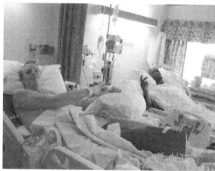

Marcus Wilson and me in NNMC Bethesda after he was injured. He had some pull since he was a senior enlisted Gunnery Sgt at the time. He asked the nurses to wheel me to his room, so that we could chat for a while. It was good to see him, but not in this condition.

When Jeff arrived at Bethesda, he had shrapnel wounds all over his face, and I think he was missing an eye. Marcus was blown up by an IED in his HMMWV twenty days after my accident; he also was the sole survivor of his accident. We lost three Marines in his accident, he lost his left leg above his knee, and he was also found by Steuter. Marcus's HMMWV was blown up and landed upside down. He was wearing his seat belt and lived. He got to Bethesda November 17th. He asked if he could see me so they wheeled me to his room on November

18th and we sat there and talked for a good while about Iraq. The best part about that day is that Marcus made me laugh. It was one of the best days I remember about Bethesda because I was able to see the guy who saved my life and see that he was still alive after his accident. It was a true blessing.

Bethesda is a big place and there are a lot of service men and women coming through with injuries. Connecting with people you actually spent time with oversees is a huge mood lifter for staying positive and working hard to recover. Because of the nature of my injuries, the days seemed to run together. Two other memories I have of Bethesda relate to my parents and the embarrassing side effect of opioid- induced constipation. My mom would drive down to Bethesda every day to sit there with me and my dad would come down on the weekends, both sitting with me for hours on end. I now see commercials on TV for a medicine that helps reduce opioid-induced constipation and I remember being constipated from being on so many pain killers. The only way I could poop was eating a McDonald's two-cheeseburger extra value meal. I got one almost twice a week just to try to be more regular!! Sorry if that's TMI (too much information), but that was a real solid memory of mine. And a very painful one.

December 8, 2006, I was released from Bethesda and was sent to an inpatient rehabilitation center, Kernan Orthopedics and Rehabilitation Hospital (now called The University of Maryland Rehabilitation & Orthopedic Institute), in Glen Burnie, Maryland. My stay would be for eleven days and I was here to learn how to walk again and to get some range of motion back in my arm. Every day I would spend hours in physical and occupational therapy. When I left Bethesda I still had internal rods and screws in my left arm and elbow. My orthopedic surgeon was hopeful that the bone would grow back and heal itself. In addition to the physical rehabilitation, I had to stay at Kernan long enough for them to take out my Jackson-Pratt drains (JP drains). These drains are little sacks that fill up with fluid from the wounds that have been operated on. During the operation, the day before Thanksgiving when the docs did skin grafts on my calf and elbow, they also did a muscle graft. They had to take part of my lat on my side and pull it up and attach it to my tricep. I have a scar that runs in a straight line from my left rib area all the way up the side of my body to my arm. It was during the muscle graft that three JP drains were inserted to collect fluid draining from the graft area and prevent infection. While waiting for the docs to remove the drains, I continued to work with my physical therapist. When she first introduced me to the parallel bars to start walking, she told me, "Listen, if you can walk between these bars I will write you a pass to go home for the weekend." That was all the incentive I needed. I was going to walk between those bars and, sooner rather than later, I was going to walk without them. I made that promise to myself in Germany. And I did it. I walked between those bars and was able to improve so much that my physical therapist said to me, "You are doing so well, we are going to discharge you for good next week. You will continue your physical and occupational therapy as an outpatient." I was somewhat surprised. Most of the people at Kernan with me were there a lot longer than I was going to be and I was prepared for a longer stay. I was discharged on December 19, 2006. I would be home for Christmas.

CHAPTER 4

The Long Walk Back

"I don't have any more moments of asking why I am still here. I do have moments where I wish that I was not here, just because my pain is so bad and I am in so much discomfort."

I was really happy to be able to go home. Being home for Christmas wasn't something I had planned for and it was a nice surprise. What no one tells you, though, is that recovery from an IED explosion doesn't stop as soon as you are discharged from the hospital or rehabilitation center. I would find out soon enough that some of my toughest days were yet to come.

December 28 was the first time I got out of the house to just go hang out with some friends. I hit up the local hang out, The Rendezvous Inn, because I knew that a lot of people who graduated from Perryville High School, my high school, went there to have drinks and listen to local music. And I was just happy to be able to be home and be around people that I knew, some of them really close friends in high school. I went back out again to the Rendezvous on New Year's Eve, and then again for my birthday on January 4, 2007. Mentally, I was starting to feel good again; happy I was home.

I was able to spend my days doing physical and occupational therapy at the Perry Point VA Medical Center. It just so happened that this, too, was right down the road from home. I met some great people there. Troy Smith was my occupational therapist and a really great guy to talk to. Alexa Shenk was one of the Physical therapists I had. She made me laugh and helped keep the smile on my face while I was there. Sue was the receptionist in the PT department, and she also helped me to laugh as I would check in and out of each appointment. My physical therapist, Dr. Peter Glover, was an Army reservist, so we hit it off well. Being around veterans helped me feel like I had a family, and the camaraderie was great. One veteran I will never forget is Mr. Floyd Earls. He was so generous and was always making me laugh. He was a great guy and would do anything to help another vet out. There was another vet we called "Ornery Amos." He was really funny and somewhat vulgar, but he would harass the therapists and always give them a hard time, so I was always smiling when he was around. It was nice seeing these vets and being able to thank them for their service to our country and for taking the same stand I did, but way before my time.

The rehabilitation staff helped me get a range of motion back in my arm, and my legs were getting stronger and stronger with physical therapy. It was during this time that I also started seeing a counselor for PTSD. Yes, I do suffer from PTSD. It is not that bad. The docs say I have a major depressive disorder more than PTSD,

but I do have some of the side effects of PTSD, such as not being able to sleep. I don't have nightmares from the accident or any of the other symptoms that would be full blown PTSD.

Something that did come up during my counseling sessions and that I hadn't discussed with anyone at this point was the survivor's guilt

Donald's gravesite and tombstone in Belmont, NY. October 2016.

I was experiencing. My survivor's guilt lasted about 7 months after the accident. It was really severe during that time. I couldn't stop questioning myself and God and asking, "Why me? Why was I the one who was kept alive?" I didn't have a family at the time. Chuck had a wife and two kids and Donald had a fiancé. I couldn't really wrap my head around why I was the one who was left here. I had an idea that God left me here to be able to share my story and that He had a great plan for my life, but it took a little while to see that. In addition to talking to a counselor at the VA, I talked to one of the pastors at my church and he helped me to clear things up in my head. He said, "What if one of the other two guys would have come back from Iraq and been abusive to their spouse," and that helped take away the constant questioning every day of why I was still here. What if Donald or Chuck saw too much over in Iraq and they couldn't cope with what they saw? What if their experiences and PTSD would have been so bad that they would have taken their own life? We have so many veterans who commit suicide every day that if I had lost Donald to suicide, my pain would be much greater. Donald was so grounded in his faith and he would always tell me that if his mom heard him talking the way he did at times when he was mad, that she would slap him in front of all of us. Knowing that these two men were in heaven rejoicing with our Lord and Savior made things a lot easier once I understood that maybe if they were left here, they would be dealing with much worse issues than I was.

I don't have any more moments of asking why I am still here. I do have moments where I wish that I was not here, just because my pain is so bad and I am in so much discomfort. The love I have for my wife and my kids keeps me from thinking about suicide. I just couldn't stand to be away from them. I can deal with the pain if I get to come home every day and see a smile on my wife and little boy's faces, and then to see the smiles on my daughters' faces when I get to see them. That makes the pain worth it every day.

My life would continue revolving around therapy: physical, occupational, and mental. Like I said before, the journey was just beginning when I was released from Kernan right before Christmas.

Fast forward to January 31, 2007. I was in the shower when I noticed a yellow discharge coming from my left elbow. I got out of the shower and called for my mom to look at my elbow. "What do you think this is?" And almost instantly my mom was walking out of the bathroom yelling, "We need to get to the emergency room right now." We hopped in the car and drove to the emergency room all the way in Bethesda (84 miles away). The ER docs admitted me right away for this new infection causing the discharge in my elbow. This infection would require another surgery to clean out the elbow wound. The follow-up from this operation also included IV antibiotics that would last for several weeks. February 12, 2007, I was released. But February 19, I was admitted again for another infection in the same elbow and stayed at Bethesda until March 1. The infection was not painful at all. What was painful was lying in the hospital and not being able to see my family and friends all the time like I was before. People would come visit, but I did not like being cooped up in a hospital room all the time. During these surgeries, they were still just going in and cleaning out the elbow and the infection. Those surgeries were not painful at all. The painful surgery was to come in May when they started to cut out the bones. By May 2007, I was back at Bethesda for treatment of my left elbow because the range of motion was still not improving.

The best way to explain what was happening with my left elbow, aside from the recurring infection, is that I was unable to get any range of motion on my own because of so many infections. The doctors were hopeful that the use of a special brace that did the bending for me and worked in conjunction with the rods and screws in my left arm would help the elbow to heal and get range of motion back on its own. My range of motion, though, was very limited in this brace to the point where I would have to bend my face all the way down to my hand if I needed to scratch it. To address the infection issues and the range of motion issues, my surgical team decided they would give me what is called a flail elbow. The surgeons would cut out the two bones that make the elbow joint and reconnect my arm with just the muscles and tendons. As a result, I can bend it all the way up and touch my face. I do have some permanent nerve problems in my left pinky finger. My ulnar nerve was cut or severely damaged in one of the many surgeries I had. Every day I deal with numbness and tingling in my left pinky. Every now and then I will experience the same kind of tingling and numbness in my forearm, too.

In June 2007, once the left elbow surgeries were complete, I went in for surgery on my left ear. I had sustained a ruptured eardrum from the explosion. The ear drum rupture was so bad that a patch wouldn't work. The doctor did a tympanoplasty and used a piece of my own tissue to do a graft that would close the hole in the eardrum. Having a blown eardrum for so long was not bad. I just would get a mute sound in my left ear every now and then. The main thing that I suffer from in the left ear now is tinnitus, a constant ringing in the ear. This comes and goes multiple times throughout the day. It is very annoying and it makes me hear things at times, too, out of the blue. But it doesn't really bother me. It is more of an annoyance that I have just learned to live with on a daily basis.

Keeping in mind that the explosion happened in 2006, as of the end of June 2007, the doctors still had not completed the surgeries necessary to repair damage to both of my knees. With a healing eardrum and a left elbow that was now recovering, my medical team set the date for my first knee surgery for September 2007. This first surgery consisted of the doctor going in and cutting out the damage to the meniscus. It helped with some of the bone-on-bone grinding, but even today, every time I walk up the stairs, both of my knees grind. Surgery on my right knee was in March 2008. It was the same procedure they did on the left knee, repairing the meniscus tear.

Finally, my doctors told me I was scheduled for my last surgery. On October 15, 2008, the surgeons used cadaver tendons to repair my anterior cruciate ligament (ACL) and my medial collateral ligament (MCL) on my left knee With the ACL and MCL tear, it caused me a lot more pain walking. While repairing the ACL and MCL, I had a pin and some screws inserted into the knee to keep the cadaver tendons in place and to keep the knee together. My orthopedic surgeon would not be able to do arthroscopic surgery this time (the way it was done on the meniscus repairs of both knees). The arthroscopic surgery is completed by making three little holes around the knee cap on the outside of the skin, one for a camera they insert into the knee, one for the tool that grinds down the cartilage, and one for a hose where they flush out the knee with water. This time my surgeon was going to be making a large incision and opening up the entire knee. The surgeon cut an incision down inside of the left knee. The crazy thing about the surgeries, though, is after the arthroscopy surgeries, I was unable to walk because the pain was a lot worse after those surgeries. After the ACL/ MCL surgery when I got home, I was able to use my crutches to walk up the steps. When I had the arthroscopic surgeries, I would have to get to the steps, turn around and sit down on the steps using my arms to push myself up each step. Then once I was in the house, I would scoot across the floor to the couch, sit down, and prop up my leg to get the pressure off my knees.

For the two years after the explosion, I had 30 surgeries and a lot of time to think about my time in the Navy. I found myself being quite reflective.

CHAPTER 5

Lost To Enlisted

"Son, I'm really proud of you. I know you're going to do well. I know you're going to make it through."

After my explosion, I wasn't sure what the future held for me. What I did learn, and learned quickly, was that I had a lot of time on my hands during my two-year recovery. I often thought a lot about why I joined the Navy and if it would even be possible to serve twenty years.

In the summer of 2003, I was 21 and I joined the Navy. I enlisted with the intent of serving 20 years. I saw it as job stability and I was growing tired of jumping from job to job. Right after high school I really wasn't sure what I wanted to do so I gained experience as a salesman in the parts department for a local Honda dealership, laying concrete, and even considered going to electrician apprenticeship school. And then I met a girl. I thought that I was in love so I was going to pick up and move across the country to be with her. As I was ready to head west, I asked her if she really wanted me to move there. The girl I thought I was so in love with let me down gently with the "I don't know if it sounds like the right time" line. By week's end, I wasn't talking to her anymore. I was talking to the Navy recruiter.

When I went to meet the recruiter, it would be easy to say it was because I had a broken heart. However, it wasn't a hard decision for me to walk through the recruiting office door. I really was tired of jumping from job to job and since 9/11, signing up to serve our country had been on my mind. The first task for me after meeting the recruiter was to take the Armed Services Vocational Aptitude Battery (ASVAB). This is a multi-aptitude series of test questions that measures your abilities and helps determine potential future job and academic success someone would have in the military. The ASVAB is conducted in testing centers across the country at Military Entrance Processing Stations (MEPS). I would take mine at Fort Meade, MD. My scores came back and I had passed my physical exam and showed the recruiters I could run a mile and a half, and pass the Navy weight standards. I had to do the 3-day diet a few times before going in to meet weight. Grapefruit is gross!! The 3-day diet consists of grapefruit and dry toast for breakfast with black tea or black coffee. I don't remember what else it was the other days, but you can find it on line. You can lose up to 10 pounds in 3 days, so I was told to do it twice the last week before I left for boot camp. Once my recruiter believed that I would meet the weight requirement and could handle the physical fitness, we got down to the business of talking about the jobs I would be best suited for. I was offered six different job possibilities. One was a storekeeper. I thought very seriously about doing that. I really did enjoy my job when I worked at the Honda dealership. I felt very comfortable with numbers, doing inventory, and doing purchase orders for materials needed for a unit. But the second job they offered me, hospital corpsman, really peaked my interest. "Tell me about this hospital corpsman stuff." And the detailer explained, "A corpsman sometimes goes with the Marines, Marine Corps Special Operations, and Special Warfare Communities as part of ground fighting units. Navy corpsmen do not just work in Naval hospitals or on board ships. They take their skills to combat zones and work side by side with the Navy and Marine Corps. Hospital corpsmen may be assigned independent duty aboard ships and submarines, Fleet Marine Force, Special Forces, and Seabee units, and at isolated duty stations where no other medical officer is available" (citation https://www.thebalance.com/hospital-corpsman-3345823). I liked what I heard and the recruiter made a great point of saying that medical training and experience will be in demand whether I stay in the Navy twenty years or leave after five. Then the recruiter mentioned that my initial contract with the Navy would be five years instead of four because corpsmen go through fourteen weeks of school before being given an assignment. My goal was still to be in the Navy for twenty years so signing for five years was just fine.

I left Maryland to go to Basic Training in November 2003. The Boot Camp, Naval Station (NAVSTA) Great Lakes and Recruit Training Command (RTC), is right on the shores of Lake Michigan, north of Chicago. Northern Illinois is freezing cold in November and I had to endure 8 weeks of boot camp.

Boot Camp was an interesting experience. I remember going to worship service on Sundays while I was in Illinois. I remember marching every single day. I remember, specifically, the first time we were marching as a unit and our chief, who oversaw our company, said, "Do you not know your right from your left, boy?" I just kept messing up the marching process. In my mind, I thought every time they were saying left, my left foot was touching. But obviously, it wasn't. I learned very quickly how to march. There was no way I wanted to be called out again.

My standard issue boot camp picture, taken around December 2003.

I came across some pretty good RDCs (Recruit Division Commanders) in Basic. My company did well throughout the entire eight weeks and we came in second place. One thing we weren't allowed to do from Basic was call home very much. The expectation was that we would write letters to family to keep them informed. For Basic Training in the Navy, each building was identified as a ship and because of that, the parts of the building were identified by the same names you would find on ships. For example, we ate in the mess hall. We would go down there and do a lot of exercising. With Basic running from November until January 30 in northern Illinois, we had a lot of snow and very cold weather. This meant that we also did a lot of exercising inside, in the mess hall or sometimes we even had to push all our bunks against the wall to make space to exercise. We marched inside, we ran inside, we even had to do two P/T tests inside. That's how cold it gets up there. Speaking of P/T tests, we did one when we first arrived and another right before graduation. We were required to run a mile and a half, do as many push-ups as we could for two minutes, and do as many sit-ups as we could for two minutes. At the time, we were required to do 44 pushups and 60 sit-ups to pass. I passed both P/T tests with flying colors.

One of the final exercises we had to complete in Basic Training was staying awake for 36 hours while working as a team to solve certain tasks. Everyone on the team is working with sleep deprivation and had to get various types of knots tied, be able to answer questions about Naval history, and perform other types of activities that required both physical and mental labor. Honestly, this exercise was just a good team building experience. It is most definitely one of the reasons why I work very well with people and get along with anybody. In our company, called a division, there were between forty and fifty of us staying in one big room in bunk beds, and there is no other option than to get along and work together as a team. Teamwork is what the military is all about. Each division is made up of so many different people of color, race, sexual orientation, culture, etc., and there is no time for drama or hate. It takes all of us to stay alive, so at Basic I learned very quickly to respect and value each person on my team. We won as a team but if teamwork failed, then we all failed miserably.

Speaking of teamwork and celebrating wins, we all watched as the SEALS caught Saddam Hussein. We were allowed to watch that on the news and I will never forget when the reporters announced

Saddam Hussein had been caught. I was out of high school when 9/11 happened and since that time I knew, at some point in my life, I would do something for the country. In high school, I didn't know that I would actually join the military. I just knew after 9/11, and because I grew up watching my grandfather serve his community as a member of his local fire department, that I would eventually do a job that served the country in some sort of way.

This was taken by my mom after I graduated from boot camp. She couldn't believe how skinny I was, so she wanted to see my stomach.

Eight weeks at Basic went by, and before I knew it, it was time to graduate. January 30, 2004, was a typical winter day in northern Illinois. It was 3 degrees, with a wind chill factor of -26 degrees. The ceremony began with all divisions marching in a relaxed state, due to the cold temperatures, to one building that could accommodate all eleven graduating divisions. All of us were in our dress blues with long coats and scarves. We even wore our facemasks and used our scarves to cover our facemasks. If we blinked while marching outside there was potential for our eyes to freeze. In Basic they taught us, when it is this cold, to breathe through your nose and out your mouth. On this day, our nose hairs froze and most of us had icicles on them. It was definitely a crazy experience in this type of cold air.

My parents and my cousin came to my graduation. It was great to see family. My mom couldn't believe how skinny I was. She thought I had withered away to nothing. Seeing my mom, especially at graduation, was an important moment in my life. Before I left for Boot Camp, my mom said one of the most hurtful things to me, actually one of the most hurtful things any child can hear from a parent. She told me that she thought I would quit Boot Camp like I quit everything else in my life (jobs and sports) up to that point. Hearing that from my mom hurt. But here we both were, on January 30, 2004, at my graduation. Honestly, what she said to me just pushed me to prove that I could do this. I told myself that her words were not going to deter me from accomplishing this great feat of graduating and becoming a Navy corpsman. My dad and I had a rocky relationship at the time. We didn't get along well. I was more of a mommy's boy and went to my mom for everything. My dad and I weren't on the best of terms. I would say we tolerated each other. But before I left for Basic, my dad took me out for a drive. I don't even remember where we were going. On that drive, an important thing happened for my dad and me. One of the last things I remember him saying to me before I left was, "Son, I'm really proud of you. I know you're going to do well. I know you're going to make it through." I needed to hear that from my dad. It was a big confidence booster and something that pushed me to want to do very well in Boot Camp. Hearing my dad say that was remarkable at the time just because of the way our relationship worked. I had a lot of pride when I graduated and it was really important to share that moment with my family. Each parent gave me exactly what I needed to hear at the right time in my life.

There was a week of time between Boot Camp and Naval Corpsman school. The neatest thing for me is that the school I was to attend was right across the street from boot camp. While I waited to be called to move across the street to Corps school, I stayed in the same ship with the same people from Basic. Those that had signed up for jobs in the air field would head to Florida for their specialty training, while the rest of us attended our job specific schools at Great Lakes, Illinois.

February 6th, 2004, I was driven in a van across the street to Corps School. I don't think I started class until March; of course, it could have been the end of February. I started a bit ahead of my class because the instructors of the Corps School had asked for volunteers. I raised my hand and I was put in another class that would be graduating a lot earlier than my originally scheduled class. I did pretty well in Corps School. Our courses consisted of a lot of anatomy and physiology. We were taught how to give shots, start IVs, how to turn a patient in bed, change bed sheets with patients in bed, and a myriad of other medical applications. Once every other week we would do PT as a class, starting at 6am, then class started at 8. We got one break in the morning, lunch was from 11-12, and then we got one more break in the afternoon and school was done at 4-4:30. After school I would either get on-line or I would go to the gym and play basketball. Sometimes I would stay up all night on-line, go to school the next day, order dinner right after school, and sleep from 5pm-5am. It was a crazy time, for sure, and I was looking forward to graduating from Corps School because I was going to get leave. On June 9, 2004, right after graduation from Corps School, I went home for two weeks.

But vacation wasn't to last very long. I had to report to field medical training in California at Camp Pendleton, where I would learn to serve with the Marines. Before classes started, I was assigned to the hospital in the Pre-Op (PACU) area. I was starting IVs on patients before they went in for surgery and I really enjoyed it. I liked being there and I liked the job. I also enjoyed wearing scrubs and not being forced to wear the Navy uniform every day. Eventually I was sent from the job in the PACU to attend classes and training for seven weeks. This is where I learned how to handle any type of casualty or trauma in the field. I was taught how to perform an endo cricoid thoracotomy by cutting a small incision in the throat and starting an airway with just an endo tube. I needed to know this in case someone's face had been blown off and they weren't able to breathe through their nose or mouth. The thoracotomy would allow them to breath. I still remember how to do this procedure. I could do it now if I had to, like if I came upon the scene of an accident. I don't carry the equipment needed to properly do one anymore, but I am sure my experience has taught me how to improvise.

While I was waiting to start classes at Camp Pendleton, I bought a motorcycle. Boy, was she a beauty. She was a 2004 Suzuki GSXR 600. I fell in love immediately with riding a bike and loved the way it felt to be on my Suzuki: riding fast, and the freedom to go from San Diego straight up to LA. I rode every single chance I got. And I was riding so much that I failed Field Med Service School (FMSS). Now I am not saying I didn't care about school. I did. I just thought I would be able to get by the way I got through Elementary through High School; memorizing everything I needed to pass the tests and maintain decent grades. FMSS didn't work that way and when I made the choice to spend my free time riding, I also was making the choice not to study and/or practice. So I failed and it meant I would have to wait to start the program all over again. The additional time it would take me to redo FMSS and pass meant that I had now been in the Navy for one year.

I got FMSS right the second time around. I put in the needed study and practice time and was relieved to graduate right before Thanksgiving in 2004. From here I would head to Downtown San Diego to go to C School (Lab Tech School). I was stationed at Naval Medical Center San Diego (NMCSD), informally known as Balboa Hospital due to its proximity to Balboa Park. I did not like Lab Tech School and could not get the microscope to focus. Because of the focusing issues really messing with my eyesight, I asked to drop the school. When I talked with the detailer, he offered me a post in Hawaii. And who would be crazy enough to miss a chance to see and live in Hawaii.

When I got to Hawaii and checked in, I found out that I would be going to 1st Battalion, 3rd Marines (1/3). At that time, they were on their way home from Iraq after being deployed to Fallujah for the Battle of Fallujah and taking back that city in 2004. While I was waiting for them to return and get back from their post deployment leave, I was working at the Regiment Aid Station (RAS). During this time, there was an Assault Amphibious Vehicle (AAV) Company who was about to deploy over to the Big Island, Hawaii, to do some training at some of the ranges out there and they needed an extra corpsman to go with them. It was June 2005, and I was told I would be going as the extra corpsman. I thought why not, and when we were there I had a great time getting to shoot some bigger guns for the first time off the AAV's, like a .742, a SAW gun, and the .50 gun. We got a weekend of liberty while we were over there, too. I went to visit Kona, where the Ironman World Championships are held every year in October. As a side note, that year I was asked if I wanted to go volunteer at the Ironman World Championships to be a medical staff person on hand. I declined, and would later kick myself in the butt for turning down the opportunity.

When I returned from the Big Island, I was placed with 1/3, my permanent unit. It wasn't long before we were getting ready to start training again for a deployment. We would deploy to Afghanistan in January 2006. During this time, I was stationed with the Headquarters and Service Company in 1/3 going into Afghanistan. During this deployment, we lost one corpsman and three Marines for the four months we were there. While there, I first went outside of the wire with an Army MP unit. They didn't have any medics stationed with them, so they used corpsmen. It was a good time, but those guys drove me crazy. They would run their HMMWV's 55mph to try to avoid getting blown up. The difference between the Army and Marines is that the Army would drive fast and not look for a fight, while the Marines drove slow and begged for someone to start shooting at them, so they could fight back.

I would deploy to Iraq with my platoon from Marine Corp Base Kaneohe. And as you already know, 2006 would be the game changer to my Naval career. Those of you with military experience know that having an injury doesn't automatically mean you are discharged. And even upon my discharge from Bethesda after the explosion, part of me was still trying to serve my country and remain in the Navy.

CHAPTER 6

Active Duty After The Explosion

"Serving with the Marines was like being in one big happy family. All of us are there for the same reason, they have your back and you've got theirs."

B ecause of the IED explosion, and spending the end of 2006 and beginning of 2007 in the hospital and rehabilitation centers, I was still officially listed as part of the battalion in Hawaii. I wouldn't receive new orders until I returned from the memorial service held in Hawaii, April 2007.

The Marines held a memorial service to honor all the guys we lost. This was before women were allowed on the front lines, so there were not any women stationed with us in Iraq. The Battalion lost a total of 23 Marines. Echo Company lost seven guys total: Lance Corporal J. S. Sandvickmonroe, First Lieutenant J. L. Booth, Lance Corporal D. B. Chaires, Lance Corporal D. S. Brown, Lance Corporal M. D. Gonzalez, Lance Corporal T. W. Brown, and Lance Corporal M. D. Scholl. I was really happy to be back in Hawaii visiting with my guys. I missed the Marines and I wanted to see as many of the guys as I could, especially Steuter. I needed to thank him for saving my life. It was easy to tell, without a lot of gushy words or gestures, that a bunch of the guys were happy to see me; I had a big crowd of them around me. My super huge smile said it all. As far as being the sole survivor of my accident, it was also important for me to see Donald's family. Donald was the gunner in my vehicle when it exploded. I knew I wouldn't get a chance to meet Chuck's family since Chuck was a Navy Reservist stationed in Montana and not a part of our unit. But the opportunity to meet Donald's family was a very special moment for me. I apologized for not being able to save him or do anything to change the course of events. Donald's parents are two of the most humble and kind people I've ever met. They were thankful that I was alive. And after time spent remembering Donald and his bravery, they both gave me a hug and told me they would continue to pray for me and my recovery.

Cpl. Steuter and me at the Memorial Service in Hawaii. I'm so grateful for him and his bravery after the IED hit the HMMWV. He immediately was looking for survivors when he found me.

My visit to Hawaii for the memorial service and a week of sightseeing with my family was a pivotal time in my life. The Marines were very good to me and my family. Yet I knew after my visit to the Battalion Aid Station (BAS) to see the guys that I was stationed with before I left and who weren't on the deployment to Iraq with me, that my injuries would change my role with the Marines. Even if the Lord blessed me and allowed me to remain enlisted as a Navy corpsman, I would never be well enough to deploy into battle with the Marines and be a part of the special brotherhood that I found in Iraq. It was a very proud moment for me when I got to reconnect with members of the Company I was stationed with in Iraq and to introduce my parents to them. I didn't know those guys that long, but as soon as we got to Iraq, we were immediately a family. That is how they treated me and how I treated them. This bond will never change. The bittersweet moment of my trip to Hawaii was realizing that, in this moment and time, I wasn't going to be able to serve with this company again.

The week in Hawaii went by very quickly. I really was sad to be saying aloha, again, to the Marines that I served with in Iraq. But there was still more work to be done on my recovery. Because I was still undergoing surgeries and rehabilitation, my station was transferred from Hawaii to Bethesda. I was asked to call in everyday and let my superiors know I was alive. There wasn't much I could do for the Navy at this point since I was still under my doctor's care.

In October 2008, I had my last surgery and was now in convalescent and rehabilitation mode. I didn't really apply for retirement. I was put into the medical board process and the Navy gave me the choice to stay in, work a desk job, and modify my Physical Fitness Test (PFT,) or get out. I wanted to get out because if I could not serve with my Marines, then I did not want to travel the world going to different Naval hospitals, working at a desk. I knew I would not be able to stay in Bethesda the full 20 years and be close to home.

I was ready to retire just because I was physically exhausted. I wanted to take time to recover at my own pace and not have to have the military guiding my recovery through physical therapy and anything else they wanted to try on me. I was so ready to retire that I didn't have any thoughts or feelings about it not being 20 years like I wanted to do. By then I was also ready to do what God had in store for me and I knew from going through the accident and what I had learned spiritually, that God had plans for me, so my time in the military needed to come to an end.

The actual medical board process began in March 2009, because the Navy needed me to recover for a certain amount of time from the last surgery on my left knee in October 2008. Once the initial recovery phase from that surgery was complete, I was able to go to all of the appointments required for the disability retirement process. It was from these appointments that doctors would document the extent of my debilitating injuries and determine what percentage I was disabled. I was not working at this time, but still in convalescent mode recovering through physical therapy at the Perry Point VAMC and making a transition into what I was going to do after the Navy. I was taking some online classes at this point through Liberty University Online. Most of these appointments were just evaluations. I saw the orthopedic doctors, psychologists, psychiatrists, general surgery doctors, and neurologists.

The entire medical board process would take one year to complete. My retirement from the Navy became official March 30, 2010. I had no idea it would take one year to complete because I was in a pilot program the military was getting ready to implement. Because of that, I honestly believed the process would have been faster. This new process was designed to allow those of us retiring the opportunity to have all of our appointments scheduled and completed in Washington, DC, at the VAMC. The goal was to streamline the process and ensure that pension checks and money from the VA would arrive sooner rather than later. But to determine the money allowed for each disability, I had to go through many appointments so the Navy could determine a percentage for how disabled I was for each injury sustained in the explosion. When all the appointments were complete and the experts could conclude that I was disabled to a point of not being able to perform my duties as assigned, I was granted a percentage of money from the military and a percentage of money from the VA. Did I mention it took one full year to complete the process? But even though it took so long, or what I felt was so long, it was nice to be able to be in this pilot program because when my official retirement date of March 30, 2010, rolled around, I received my first check from the VA on May 1, 2010. I had to appeal the process from the Navy at first. When my first Navy evaluation came back, they declared me to be 10% disabled from the military and 70% from the VA. I was fine with the 70% from the VA, but from the Navy, I was hoping to retire medically to receive some of the benefits for the rest of my life, such as Tricare health insurance at a very low annual rate. But for that I needed to be retired at least at 30% disability. I fought and appealed to the Med Board and after they looked everything over again, they came back and gave me a 40% disability rating. I was okay with that so I took that percentage and ran. I would eventually continue to add more claims to my VA disability and get to 100%, but it would take a little over 2 years to get there.

I did not have a plan in place for a job when I started the Med Board process. My disability pay would not cover all of my expenses so I needed to get out there and find a job. I also knew that if I were to sit home and just collect disability, I would be quite miserable. For my own sanity, I needed to get out of the house and interact with people. A friend of mine at church put me in contact with a retired state trooper who was working for a security company, Pinkerton Government Services (PGS). PGS had just been awarded the contract to keep security at the Northrop Grumman facilities around BWI airport and they were getting ready to conduct training my last week of active duty with the Navy. I started going through that training right before my retirement. I started working at Northrop Grumman with Pinkerton right around the first of April. I was blessed that things fell right into place and I was thankful to be able to have a job. It was a huge relief to have income coming in while things were transferring from the military over to the VA.

The thing I miss the most about the Navy and being with the Marines is the camaraderie. Serving with the Marines was like being in one big happy family. All of us are there for the same reason; they have your back and you've got theirs. That is one of the reasons so many military veterans have a hard time adjusting to the outside civilian world – there is no camaraderie like there is in the military. In your unit everyone is so close; you do everything together during the day. They become your closest friends. Even though we may not hang out together on the weekends, we are still together a lot. During deployments, the unit is together 24/7. That doesn't happen in the civilian world. And when something like what happened to me happens, civilians have a really hard time understanding what you went through. Civilians become more distant from you and you tend to close people off. It feels like no one can understand because they haven't been in the military. For me, I really wanted people to ask so I could explain it, but the flip side of that is that civilians don't ask because they don't want to make me live through it again. That cycle repeats itself until you end up with no friends besides your family, unless you cut them off for various reasons. Today, if it wasn't for my wife, I wouldn't have very many friends and people we get together with. If I lived closer to the two Marines who saved my life, then it would be different for me. I would be getting together with them all of the time. They know exactly what I went through and understand the camaraderie. Doing it through text messages isn't the same thing. And checking in every month or two isn't the same as being able to see them. I owe those men everything that I can give them. If they need something, then I want to help them through it and help them try to fix it. I am a fixer; that is my personality and what I enjoy doing. I enjoy helping people; it's part of my nature and who God made me to be. So the camaraderie is what I miss the most.

Another thing I miss is being able to travel somewhere new and see another part of the world every three years or so when my detail was up. But because of my injuries, I just didn't want to stay in and have to worry about trying to keep up with PT. Especially since I didn't know what kind of limitations I was going to have after my recovery.

And then there are things I do not miss. I don't miss living in a barracks and having to do "Field Day" every Thursday to get your room and barracks ready for Friday morning inspection. Field Day is when the whole barracks gets together every Thursday night to clean everything to be able to have it inspected Friday morning. If we passed inspection then we were granted liberty for the weekend. Field Day was never any fun. I don't miss the rationed food. The food never really did anything for me. There were some meals I liked, but the majority of them were not very good. I also don't miss having to wear a uniform every day. Some of the uniforms were uncomfortable, the camouflage uniforms we got to wear with the Marines were the most comfortable uniforms I wore, but having to get them cleaned and make sure they all looked good all the time was a nuisance. We were expected to have our uniforms available for inspection at any time. Thankfully, being with a unit that deploys all the time, we didn't have time to keep our uniforms inspection-ready and they never came around and checked them either. Thank goodness, because I gained weight and probably wouldn't have fit in much of my uniforms at that time.

My life as a Navy corpsman changed me. I don't regret making the decision to join the Navy and I don't regret making the choice to retire due to medical disability. I am proud of the man I am today and I know, without any doubt, my time with the Navy and my Marine brothers lent itself to making me a man of honor.

The next section of my book will focus on my faith. It is important to my story that I have been saved by the grace of God and that God always is the right path to take. Things were not always easy for me and I didn't always make the best choices as a kid and as an adult, but declaring Jesus as my Lord and Savior has given me a chance to grow and have a strong family together where He is front and center.

CHAPTER 7

Visions And Resolve

"My Pastor anointed me with oil and prayed for God's protection upon me."

L et me tell you about a crazy story from before I left for Iraq. I was home on leave before shipping out, and I used the time at home to also visit and worship at my local church. This is the church where I accepted Jesus as my Lord and Savior and it will always have a special place in my heart. Prior to arriving home, I'd been under a lot of attack from Satan and I just wasn't my normal self. I honestly had these visions that I was not going to make it home alive from Iraq.

Throughout my life there were different times growing up that I didn't think I would live to see a certain age. There was a time when I was in high school that I didn't think I was going to live to see 21. I am talking about the kind of visions that are so vivid and real, that when I would wake up in the morning I had to double check current events, the calendar, and my family to make sure the visions did not really happen.

The first chance I had to attend a church service once getting back to Maryland, I went because I wanted to talk to my pastor. I needed to share with someone who would understand, without question, the visions I was having about dying in Iraq. When the pastor did his altar call during the service, I went up front. The pastor called up some of the men in the church, the deacons, to pray over me. My pastor anointed me with oil and prayed for God's protection upon me while I was serving in Iraq. I know, without doubt, the anointing of the oil and the prayer for protection gave me the resolve to keep my life centered on God while I was in Iraq. And as my journey through the explosion and recovery would soon follow, it became clear that a big reason that God kept me alive, and kept me here on earth, was to be able to tell my story and share my testimony with others.

I was 24 years old on the day of my accident. It was, and still is, a humbling experience for me to have survived the explosion. I heard God say to me, "Son, I have plans for you. I'm going to use you, your testimony, and your story to help others." In Iraq, I really started to see God daily. I know He was with me every day because I worked hard to maintain my relationship with Him. My first day in Iraq, I heard a bullet bounce off my vehicle for the first time. And it was a scary sound. That night I started getting back into my Bible reading, praying, and participating in the group prayer before we went on every single convoy. I made a vow to God on that day to make time each day for reading and praying. And I made a promise to listen for His guidance. We had a guy from Texas that was with us in Iraq who was a minister. He always made sure to pray over us and give us a little verse, a prayer, and positive words. I am blessed to have served in the military and come home with all my limbs, my sight, and the ability to start and maintain a family. For God to keep me here is just remarkable. Especially since I had not always lived my life for God. He still found a way to my heart during my early days in the Navy and pulled me out of that muck and clay that I was living in. It was as if He took me out to the woodshed and gave me the beating that I needed just to see how real and how powerful He is. He spoke to me of His plans for all His children. When I chose to hear and really listen to God, I was mind blown. And I became thankful and appreciative every day for the life that I have here on this earth.

Being thankful didn't come easy to me after the explosion. It was just so crazy to me that I was still here. I had quite a few times, right after the explosion, where I had extreme survivor's guilt. I questioned God, "Why me? Why me? Why did you leave me here? Why didn't you leave these other guys?" My buddy, Donald, who actually was my rack mate, was the one that was in the turret. He had gotten engaged some time before deployment. His fiancé flew out to Hawaii and he asked her to marry him on the beach. Donald told me all about his proposal and how lucky he felt to be marrying the girl of his dreams. I didn't have anybody in particular in my life. And the other guy killed in the explosion, Chuck, had two kids and a wife back in Montana. All I could do was keep asking, "God, why me?"

The survivor's guilt really felt like a huge burden and weight on my shoulders. It was a very deep kind of depression where I was constantly reminded of the accident. Satan kept trying to tempt me by putting thoughts and voices in my head to convince me that God didn't love me. I found myself asking, "If He did love me, then why did He let me go through this, etc." I squashed those thoughts and voices from Satan by reading my Bible and reading certain passages that really helped me know why I was still here.

CHAPTER 8

My Road To Salvation

"God loves you so much."

Walking with God is a daily journey that requires hard work. I cannot say that I have always been a Christian because I didn't accept Jesus as my Lord and Savior until I was in ninth grade. But I will say that God has always had a hand on me. His love for me has never waned; I just needed to open my heart to see His work in my life.

I grew up living in a trailer park that had another smaller trailer park adjoining it through a field. We had a two-bedroom trailer with one bathroom and it was fine for us. I remember there being so many kids to play with. My first friend in the trailer park was a boy named Ryan and we first met when we were 5 years old. My brother, Phillip, and I were outside playing and Ryan was riding his bike around the area in front of our house. To the left of our trailer, in the front, was a speed bump and Ryan's grandparents' trailer also had a speedbump in front of it. Ryan and his sister were at their grandparents a lot and the general rule of thumb, at that age, was that he could ride his bike between the two speed bumps. So we met and became instant friends as we road our bikes together between two speed bumps.

Once we started kindergarten, we were able to play together more. We would ride our bikes, play hide and seek, play in the mud puddles when it rained, and all kinds of other activities. I don't remember what age I was when Ryan moved away to Virginia, but I remember being very sad to lose my first friend.

My next-door neighbors used to babysit my brother and me a lot. Their names were Belinda Smith and Bernetta Blackburn; both had brothers. Belinda's brother was Bubby Smith and Bernetta's brother was David Blackburn. As a kid I really looked up to those two guys. I was always asking them to play ball, or ride their bikes with me around the entire trailer park, or anything else I could get them to do. Another neighbor, Brian Mott, was the first person I knew who joined the military. He went into the Air Force shortly after high school and I was around him a lot. Brian had a python as a pet and I loved holding it. When he first got it, it was just a little tiny thing, maybe like 6 feet in length. By the time he left for the Air Force, it was between 15 and 18 feet long. Brian was a great guy; he would give you the shirt off his back and help you in any way he could. Hanging around him really helped me to learn how to treat people. He was always smiling and just watching him interact with people is one of the reasons I am who I am today. I always try to keep a smile on my face and I am always willing to help someone. Knowing Brian and watching him succeed in the Air Force was a contributing factor to my decision to join the military.

I met my best friend through middle and high school when we were in seventh grade. Kelly Backert and I were close as friends. Close enough to exchange Christmas and birthday gifts. In my eighth-grade yearbook, Kelly wrote, "God loves you so much." By the time we started ninth grade, Kelly and I were spending a lot more time together and in the spring of 1997, I started to go to church with her and her family. Kelly was someone with an amazing upbeat personality and was always happy, no matter what day-to-day trials she might have been experiencing. I wanted that for me. I didn't see myself as an upbeat, positive person, and I definitely wasn't happy all the time. I knew a part of me was missing something.

I started attending church as often as I could. I would go to different services and try to absorb as much as I could. There was a lady in my trailer park I knew well. She and a couple of older ladies would let me ride with them to church for the early service at 8 am. I would stay for the 9:30 Sunday School class and find myself back in the pew for the 10:30 to noon service. I liked being at church so much and liked being around everybody that was at church. I just had a good time being there.

It was Easter Sunday, March 30, 1997, and I was at church for the early service. I was sitting by myself near the ladies that I rode with, but none of my other friends were there in that service at the time. The pastor gave the altar call and something happened to me. I was being led by the Holy Spirit to answer God's call for my salvation. Without hesitation, I walked up front and I said, "Pastor I need to be saved." I said it loud enough that those sitting in the second row could hear me ask to be saved. I wasn't playing around because I knew that the Lord was calling me for salvation. I didn't have to ask any questions because I had been going to the church for a while and seeing people give their lives to Christ. I knew what I needed and that was Jesus in my heart. I was taken upstairs by a Deacon named John Taylor. Together we talked through some things and he led me through a prayer for my salvation. Immediately afterwards I felt so much love and joy in my heart. I felt this overwhelming amount of abundant love and I just had so much love to give. I just wanted to share that love with people.

CHAPTER 9

Faith and Potholes

"Thank God for His hedge of protection upon me."

For a week or so after I got saved, I felt different. I still had the abundant amount of love and joy in my heart but other things were going on as well. I was a freshman in high school. I had friends that I wanted to also please and so trying to walk with Christ and lead others to Him made me stand out. And in high school I wanted to fit in. I started doing what I wanted to do and the things that made me feel good. Some of my friends didn't make great choices and I went along for the ride. I smoked marijuana pretty much throughout high school (except for about a year after I was saved). I started smoking pot again because I just wanted to blend in and feel happy. It felt like I was cool and pot really relaxed me. I would smoke with my friends and get the giggles. If I could keep my friends laughing then they would keep me around.

As high school graduation was getting closer, I had to take a final exam for Advanced Placement (AP) English. Now, the only reason I was taking AP English was because Maryland required all seniors to take an English class in their senior year. For some reason when my senior year started, I wasn't assigned an English class. When the guidance department realized the mistake, I was put into AP English because it was the only class left with space in it. I didn't want to be in the class and the teacher knew I shouldn't have been in the class. But I was, and both of us were stuck with each other. With the exam coming up, I found myself feeling plagued by senioritis. I didn't care about school at this point, and to top it all off, I was sick as a dog with some sort of stomach bug. I missed several days of school but had to drag myself in for the AP English final. My graduation was dependent on taking and passing this final. In a pair of sweatpants and a t-shirt I took the exam. Needless to say, I didn't do well. The "D" on the final exam was good enough, though, to pass the course with a "C" and graduate.

High School graduation was in June 2000. In Maryland there is a tradition of heading down to Ocean City, Maryland for Senior Week after graduation. For most seniors it is the first time away from home without adult supervision. I was no exception, and I was really looking forward to this week. Not only was I going to be away from home without adult supervision, but I was also living my life, doing what I wanted, without Christ front and center.

It wouldn't take long before I would realize that God had different plans for me. As soon as we got to Ocean City, Maryland, I bought marijuana and I smoked a little bit before going to a free concert they were having on the beach. Jimmy's Chicken Shack and Run DMC were performing and I was bound and determined to get a spot in the front row. As soon as I secured my spot up close and personal to the stage, I had this overwhelming feeling like I was going to pass out. I tried to flag somebody over to buy some water, but with such a large crowd, no one saw me. I had to back away from the stage and I had to walk down to First Street to get something to drink. Sweat was pouring off me and I was turning white as a ghost. There was no way I would be able to go back to the concert and so I decided to walk from First Street back to my hotel on Tenth Street. I staggered up the boardwalk and was very lucky that I didn't get stopped for being intoxicated. At that time, I was not drunk but I was high on something. To this day I am not sure what was in that marijuana but it really messed me up.

There is a reason I am telling you this story. As I mentioned earlier, I wasn't really living my life for Christ through most of high school. But on that day in Ocean City, Maryland, right after graduation, God was watching over me. I made it back to my hotel room and I slept for 18 hours. And once I started feeling better, I decided right then and there to stop smoking pot and start getting myself back into church.

Now that high school was over, it was easier for me to grow in my faith and become more involved in my church. Although I was still working and living in the area where I went to high school, I didn't see my friends every day. When we did get together, we weren't sitting around smoking weed.

I made the decision to move into my grandmother's house (my mom's mom) in 2001. She lived just a couple miles from us and I really wanted to move out of the trailer and have my own room. I am thankful God got me out of there when he did because events transpired afterwards that could have had a huge impact on my future.

This is really hard for me to talk about, but I was not happy living at my parent's house. Philip, my brother, had just graduated from high school and was always smoking pot. Since we shared a room, my clothes and room always smelled like marijuana. I stopped smoking it over a year before this and did not want to be around marijuana anymore. I talked to mom about it, and she said that she didn't want Philip to get in trouble by doing it outside, so she wasn't going to make him stop using it in the house. I was fed up and left. I stopped in front of our trailer when I left because it faced the main road. I dumped the clutch in my car and burnt out in front of the house. I went and talked to my grandmother, who lived a few miles away and asked her if I could move into her house. She said that I could, so I moved within a day or two. This move was something that I can look back on now and thank God for his hedge of protection upon me.

After I moved out, I would still go to my parent's house after I got off work at 10pm and get on their computer. I would stay there until 2 or 3 in the morning just chatting with people and making internet friends before social media was a thing. This wasn't the best use of my time, but it was entertaining and I enjoyed talking to people and meeting new people, no matter where they were from.

A few weeks after I moved out, my mom had a friend come visit her from San Francisco. I don't know the truth of the matter and probably never will, but my mom was being watched by the cops. Supposedly, she was having her friend send her crystal meth through the mail and my mom was selling it in the area. That is what she was arrested for and accused of, but I do not know the truth of what happened. For this I am thankful, because I know it was probably in my best interest. My mom and her friend had gone to a Madonna concert in Philadelphia; I went to her house after work to get on the computer and was there late. My mom and her friend got home after I left. When they got home, my mom made crab soup and brought it to my grandmother's house the next morning. While my mom was there, the cops showed up at her house and ransacked the place looking for drugs. That morning there was marijuana in the room my brother and I shared, for him to sell or get rid of. Had I been living there at the time, I would have been sleeping from being up so late. I would have either been arrested for the drugs or at least detained, and God knows what would have happened when the cops wanted information from me that I did not have.

They found crystal meth in the house, inside my mom's friend's suitcase, and the friend denied it was hers. My mom was arrested and taken to the Cecil County Detention Center for the night. When I got off work, I had no idea this had happened. I walked into the house through the back door, and saw that there were clothes thrown all over my parents' bed, and my dad was putting things away. He said, "I wouldn't go out there if I were you." I asked him, "Why?" He said, "I just wouldn't." So I walked out to the living room to attempt to get on the computer and it was gone. When the cops were there, they also confiscated the computer. I walked back and asked my dad what was going on and he told me that the cops were there that day and my mom had been arrested. I took off work the next day to go with my dad to get my mom out of the detention center and help him with whatever he needed that day. My mom went to trial and was given 18 months of supervised probation. My parents were evicted from the trailer park, and they moved in with my grandmother and me. My brother moved to Perryville with my other grandparents.

I cannot thank God enough for getting me out of my parents' house when He did, because my career could have been ruined. Had I been there that day when all of this went down, I could have a permanent record, drug charges on my record, and I would not have been able to join the Navy or be a nurse. God was definitely looking out for me during this time in my life. I don't hold any grudges or animosity towards my parents for this incident. I wish I knew the whole truth, but I am sure it is in my best interest not to know. I'm thankful for God's protection from this incident so that He could set me up for what He had in store for me all along.

CHAPTER 10

Answering The Call

"I felt in the very depths of my soul, that the Holy Spirit was leading me to answer the call to be a preacher."

My church family gave me a solid foundation on which to build my faith in Christ. After I gave up smoking marijuana and settled into life after high school, moving in with my grandmother and working to make a living, I started attending church again on a regular basis. Through my involvement in my church and allowing God to be at the forefront of my life, I felt like I was being called into the ministry to become a preacher. It was October, 2002, and I answered another altar call at the end of the service. I was 20 years old, and I felt in the very depths of my soul that the Holy Spirit was leading me to answer the call to be a preacher. I was being led to the altar to let my Pastor and church know that I was answering the call. I admired my Pastor a lot and really looked up to him. Over the next several months, we talked frequently and together we started looking into different colleges and universities that I should visit.

During this time of exploration into schools, I also was doing a lot of soul searching with my Pastor to prepare for the next chapter in my life. On my 21st birthday, I delivered my first sermon during Sunday evening service. My sermon was based on Proverbs 26:11, "As a dog returns to his vomit so a fool returns to his folly." The idea came to me for the sermon because of a Christian concert I had attended in the summer of 2002. The message the band shared was geared around this verse and it really stuck with me as a 20-year-old kid. At 20 years old, I was constantly at war with the world and all of its temptations versus living my life as a Christian and following God.

I knew that I was supposed to be living my life as a Christian, following God's plan and being obedient. And when I heard Proverbs 26:11, it resonated with me. This is what I have done time and time again. I would just turn back on God and turn to worldly ways, whether it be using foul language or just not honoring God with my actions. And from that verse, my sermon was born.

I used one of the stories from the concert I attended. The guys in the band explained Proverbs 26:11 like this, "Think about a couple who owns a nice house with a formal living room. The type of room with expensive furniture that is only used when guests come over. But the family dog doesn't know that the room is for guests only. He goes into the living room and throws up all over the floor. Before the couple can clean it up, the dog is back in the room eating his own vomit (as dogs do). This is what it is like for Christians trying to follow God every day. In daily life we all struggle to do what is right instead of turning back towards worldly things." I felt like a fool because I would go back to living this worldly life, doing these worldly things, and try to be a Christian at the same time. I talked about other times in the Bible where people just didn't listen to God. I spoke of Lot being called out of Sodom and Gomorrah and God raining down fire and brimstone in the city. He told Lot and his family not to look back on the city or else they'd be turned into a pillar of salt. Lot's wife didn't abide by that and she got turned into a pillar of salt because she turned and looked back. That's what people do as Christians. That's what people do in their everyday lives. They just turn back to the things that are unhealthy for them.

My sermon was received well and I felt really close to the Lord. I was growing as a Christian every day and was eager to learn new things from my Pastor and from the Bible. I completed my college visitations and I decided that I would attend Tennessee Temple University in Chattanooga, Tennessee, to study to become a preacher.

But as a fool returns to his folly, I, too, turned back to a worldly life. I never enrolled at Tennessee Temple University. During the summer leading up to starting school in the fall, I met a girl and lost my virginity. I committed a sin and felt like I wasn't worthy enough to preach anymore. It felt like I had just given away my dignity and the purity that I had for the Lord. And I had made a vow in high school, during a True Love Waits retreat, to practice abstinence until I was married. I broke my own vow and that really had a big impact on me and my self-esteem. Making matters worse, I never talked to anybody, including my pastor, about committing this sin. Instead, I just walked away from God and His calling me to become a preacher. It was that summer I signed up to join the Navy.

CHAPTER 11

Finding My Balance

"There was only one perfect person to walk the earth. That was Jesus Christ himself. As Christians, it's not about living a perfect life. It's about knowing Jesus Christ as your personal Lord and Savior and being in constant communication with Him."

As I grew in character during my time as a Navy Corpsman, so, too, did I grow in my faith. I would continue to feel the struggle between walking with Christ and turning back to living in a materialistic world.

Earlier I talked about my military history, the IED explosion, and what happened afterward. It is important to understand those events in order to appreciate the relationship I have with my Lord and Savior and being called to share my story.

After signing up with the recruiter to join the Navy, I was still going to church. I just wasn't going on a regular basis. I was carrying a lot of guilt over losing my virginity before getting married, and I was transitioning from wanting to be a pastor to being a Navy corpsman.

Getting off the bus at basic training was a far cry from going to Tennessee Temple University. I remember walking off the bus and immediately having people yell at us. They were screaming for us to get in line, start walking, take our clothes off, change into the Navy uniform, grab this, grab that, etc. The yelling didn't stop and I was not prepared for it. Since I was going to Chicago I was wearing a heavy Columbia parka-type jacket. When we were being yelled at to underdress, I put my coat down in the hallway and forgot to pick it up when moving onto the next station. I asked if I could go get it and they told me no. So I lost my favorite jacket. It dawned on me that I was sleep deprived from all of the rushing around to get to the airport and then on to the bus to get to boot camp. Everything was rush, rush, rush.

It took me a couple of weeks before I actually started going to church services. On Sundays, we had the opportunity to either sit and write letters back home, or we could go to church. In the beginning of boot camp, I wanted to write home as much as I could and to catch up on sleep so much that I didn't make it to church. After a few weeks, I settled into a routine and started going to a church service on base. Getting back into church actually helped me get through boot camp.

The services each Sunday helped me to focus my mind on also honoring and serving the Lord. But there were times when frustration would kick in and I would turn away from God. Looking back to those times, I wish I had made some different choices and stuck with Sunday church services, but I am not perfect. There was only one perfect person to walk the earth. That was Jesus Christ himself. As Christians, it's not about living a perfect life. It's about knowing Jesus Christ as your personal Lord and Savior and being in constant communication with Him. It's a relationship that's like a marriage. You have to have communication. You have to be honest with one another. You have to put the other person first. And that's what Christianity is like. It's a working relationship where it won't always be perfect, but making the choice to be in a relationship with Jesus Christ means setting time aside every day to make sure the relationship is growing. It is my faith in God that gets me through each day. It means saying my prayers at night time before going to bed, in the morning, and whenever I need strength to be able to get through the moment.

I made it through boot camp and headed across the street to Navy Corpsman School where I met some guys from a church in Indiana. The guys introduced me to the First Baptist Church in Hammond, Indiana. It was just outside of Chicago across the state line. Also in Hammond was Hyles Anderson College, a Christian college affiliated with First Baptist Church of Hammond. The college students would work on bus ministries. One of the bus ministries was to come up to the base and run intramural sports for the service men and women. In the fall we played football, in the winter it was basketball, and in spring and summer it was softball.

Because I arrived in the winter, I started playing basketball with the church group every Saturday evening. Afterwards we, the service men and women, would go spend the night at someone's home, similar to a host home, with either a college student and their family or one of the other men and their wives from the church. We would wake up on Sunday morning and have a nice, home-cooked meal before heading to Sunday services together. It was an amazing fellowship opportunity and I did it every weekend. Spring rolled around and we switched from basketball to softball. I was growing in my faith. These young guys, who were around my age or older, showed me that I didn't have to sacrifice my faith while serving in the Navy. I just enjoyed being around these college students, growing my faith, and learning how to balance my time so I was able to hold God front and center.

My faith and work-life balance was in tip top shape while I was at corpsman school. But things would change once I was transferred to California. Remember that I said every day requires a renewed commitment to God? And just like Proverbs 26:11 said it would happen, I returned again to worldly living. The first thing I did when I got to California was to buy a motorcycle. Having a motorcycle meant that attending church was very much in question. I didn't have a lot of free time and when I did, I was on my bike.

All I did was ride my motorcycle every day that I could. Any and every day I would take my motorcycle out and just enjoy the freeway. I could drive along the coast and enjoy all the beauty California had to offer. I would go to Los Angeles and cruise through Hollywood and Rodeo Drive. One weekend I rode out to Phoenix. My motorcycle gave me freedom and access to places I had never been.

While I was in California I never really went to church. I never found a church that I could attend. My faith just kind of slipped to the wayside. I wasn't growing as a Christian. I wasn't reading my Bible on my own. I was just riding my motorcycle.

Things didn't change for me even in Hawaii. I still wasn't spending time trying to find a church to attend regularly. I spent my time meeting people but once my motorcycle arrived from California, I was on it as much as I could be.

God has a way of making his presence known and He found me struggling in my faith when I was deployed the first time to Afghanistan. I always took my Bible whenever I moved or was deployed and I did start to do some reading while I was overseas. But truth be told, I was spending more of my time watching movies and listening to music. I was really just looking for an escape that didn't cause me to think too much.

When I got back from Afghanistan I couldn't sleep. I had a severe case of insomnia and instead of turning to God, I started drinking. In a three-and-a-half-month period, I spent over a thousand dollars on booze. For me, this was crazy, ridiculous behavior and it wouldn't be long before God helped me realize I had a drinking problem.

Doing some studying and reading while on deployment in Afghanistan in January-May 2006.

I was fortunate enough to be able to return home to Maryland before my deployment to Iraq. I said before that I was under attack from Satan and feared that I wasn't going to make it home alive. I didn't understand what these feelings were or why they were coming to me. I was scared and wanted to talk to my pastor. My pastor called a group of men together to come and pray over me to ask for protection while I was in Iraq, and that God's will be done. My mind was put to ease and once I got to Iraq, I started looking at my Bible a lot more. Being scared was an understatement, and my safety net was reading the Bible and praying every day. The first time I heard a bullet bounce off the steel of the Humvee and realizing we were being shot at every time we left base, was scary and crazy. The only thing I knew was to turn to God to ease my mind and my spirit. I needed to be sure that I was right with God. I really didn't want to die and be sent to hell because my relationship wasn't right with God. I will say, looking back on this time in my life, I've come to the point of knowing now that once we ask for salvation, we can't really ever lose it. We don't lose salvation as long as we mean it and as long as we're doing what we're supposed to be doing for the Lord. I didn't learn that until after my accident.

When I arrived in Bethesda after the explosion, I was more alert and more aware of everything that happened. I started praying more and reading my Bible to seek some understanding as to why I was still here. I asked folks from my home church in Maryland to come and visit me. When they came to visit, they would pray with and for me. Sometimes they would read the Bible to me because I was so weak from the explosion. I was reminded by this fine group of people that what had happened was God's will and God's plan for me, and that my testimony would serve as a vehicle to help others. With their help, I came to understand what my purpose is in this life. It's my calling to be able to try to help people. Throughout this time of physical recovery, I was also undergoing my spiritual recovery by finding my way back to the Lord. When I could finally attend church services at my home church, I found myself at ease and eager to learn. I knew that I wanted to have a family and to be able to teach my kids that God can get them through anything. I also knew I wanted to provide a strong foundation of faith and give them the skills and tools they would need to succeed in life.

CHAPTER 12

Faith and Family

"On July 3, 2015, I married the best friend I've ever had."

The entire time I was recovering from all the surgeries I was having, with physical therapy, and counseling for PTSD, I was growing closer to God. I could feel His presence in my life. My life verse, the verse I go to for daily living, is Matthew 5:8, "Blessed are the pure in heart, for they will see God." When my focus is on keeping my heart pure and full of God's love and will, I can see God working in people's lives and that's how I see God. That's how I know He's really with me. That's how I feel and that's how I understand Him speaking to me. When I pray, I ask, "Lord, how can I really honor and glorify you with the testimony you have given me?" And when I focus on keeping my heart pure, I can hear and feel His will for me.

Try as I might to keep God front and center, I got depressed when my previous marriage ended. It was less about the actual marriage and more because I had two beautiful daughters and I was very sad that I wouldn't be seeing them every day. During this time I had a choice to make: I could go and listen for God, or I could turn away from my faith (this would have been the easier choice since I was questioning why God would let this happen to me). I chose to turn towards God and sought the help of a therapist. I needed to learn how to be happy wlth myself.

My faith and regular attendance in church kept me grounded through this life transition. It would be this focus on my spiritual recovery that would lead me to find the perfect wife for me.

On July 3, 2015, I married the best friend I've ever had. It was a perfect setting; sunrise on the beach. We didn't need all the bells and whistles that come with big weddings, we just needed each other. We each agree that it was the best day of our lives. God is front and center in our relationship and to understand how He brought us together, I want to share a bit about our history. Jenn and I played together as kids, and our families have a history together that goes back to when our grandfathers were just teenagers.

Tybee Island, GA on our wedding day, July 3,2015. I married my best friend.

My grandfather and Jenn's grandfather, Bill Knell, were good friends through the community fire department. They both joined at a young age and served together for 50+ years. I remember one of the first concerts I went to was with my grandparents. We went to see Reba McIntire and Jenn's grandparents went with us. As a result of this lifelong friendship, I met Jenn when we were very young. Her parents ended up moving to the trailer park where I was living with my parents and brother, Philip, when she was 3. They moved out nine years later, but there were a few times we played together in those early years. One Christmas, I got a red remote control (RC) truck. Later that winter we had a snow storm and I drove my RC truck down to her house and we played in the snow. I helped her and her sister build a snow tunnel, and showed off my RC truck by driving it on top of the snow. In typical 90s fashion, Jenn's mom recorded a home video of this. I haven't seen this video because no one has a VHS player anymore, but Jenn swears it exists. That snow storm is one event that sticks out for both of us; outside of that we didn't spend too much time together as kids. Never in my imagination did I ever think that God would bring us together in marriage over 20 years later.

Once I graduated from elementary school and moved on to middle school, I would not see Jenn very often until high school. I was 3 grades ahead of her, so when I was a senior, she was a freshman. I would say hello when I saw her in the hallway at school, but I was only in school half a day back then. Once I graduated I didn't stay in touch with Jenn. I did not have her AOL Instant Messenger name, so I was not in touch with her again until I requested to be her friend on Facebook in 2014. Jenn informed me recently that we were connected on MySpace before Facebook was made available to the general public. This was not long after my accident, so I'm not surprised that I don't remember. After reconnecting on social media after my separation, I asked her out. I wanted to meet up with her to chat and see if we'd be able to connect on anything other than both being divorced. That was October 29, 2014. Jenn will tell you that throughout the night she couldn't read me that well. I remember we watched the World Series at a local bar and we smiled and just talked. At times, we would watch the game and there were moments of silence, but we talked a lot about what we had been through in the past. At the end of the night Jenn will tell you that I gave her an awkward side hug and she didn't know how things were going to pan out. I don't remember the awkward side hug, but I knew I liked her and wanted to continue seeing her.

I am including a special excerpt here written by Jenn. As we all know, women remember much more than guys when it comes to first dates and such.

Everything Larry has said about our childhood is just the way I remember it. I do have a few memories he doesn't have, though. For starters, I remember the day I found out that he had been hit by an IED in Iraq. I was in college, but had been visiting my Granny when his grandmother called asking for prayers for Larry. I remember Granny telling me everything she knew, which wasn't much. I remember feeling scared for the friend I had as a child, and I remember praying that he would be okay. He was the first person I knew that had been injured in the war, and he was all over the local news in the coming days and weeks. I remember connecting with him on MySpace and wanting to reach out on a personal level, but changing my mind because I was in college and he was dealing with his recovery. We were in two very different places in our lives, but to say I could kick myself now for not reaching out back then would be an understatement.

Fast forward to the new wave of social media. It could have been 2014 or it could have been sooner, I don't remember. I don't remember which one of us sent the friend request, but I do remember being "friends" for a while before he reached out via Facebook Messenger. I was surprised to hear from him after so much time, but

was happy to reconnect with someone I always considered to be a genuinely nice guy. The first few messages we exchanged are still in my message list on Facebook. Every now and then I go back and read them again and find myself laughing at how it all transpired.

Anyway, two days after that first message we went out to the Pickled Herring Pub in North East, MD. He wanted to meet me for dinner and

Red Sox-O's game in Baltimore. Jenn and I have a love-hate relationship during baseball season.

offered to drive closer to where I was working, outside of Washington, D.C., but dinner seemed like too big of a commitment for a first date. Even though I knew him previously, I didn't want to be stuck sitting through a meal with someone if the date didn't go well. It's much easier to leave the bar without a big explanation. I arrived first, and sat at the bar instead of a small table. Again, less commitment. When he finally arrived, he had the biggest smile on his *face. That immediately put me at ease. Thankfully, the World Series was on and we are both baseball fans, so we could watch the game some without worrying about carrying on a conversation the entire night. As we sat there, he was hard to read. One minute he had great eye contact and seemed to be super interested in me and our conversation, and the next minute he seemed to be all over the place. I honestly didn't know sitting there if there would be a second date. (I learned later that this was just his personality as a people watcher). When we eventually left, he walked me to my car, offered an awkward side hug, and said goodbye. Once again, I thought to myself that there probably wouldn't be another date. Later that night, we texted some and ended up talking on the phone for a couple of hours. That phone call changed my mind about seeing him again, and from that night until we moved in together not a day passed that we didn't speak. Every weekend that he didn't have his girls was spent together, and on the weekends he did have them, we'd grab a late dinner after their mom picked them up. I moved to Howard County two weeks after we started dating, and he was still in Oxford, PA, so it was difficult to see each other during the week. We were committed to a weekly date night, and decided to meet in the middle every Wednesday for dinner. Having to rely on our daily phone calls forced us to open up and really get to know one another better. We probably learned more in a few short months than most people learn over the course of a few years. There wasn't anything we didn't talk about, but most importantly, we ended each call by reading our Bibles and praying together.*

One of the things we both wanted out of a relationship was for it to be God-centered. We wanted to make sure we put God first in everything we did, so we started reading and praying together, giving each other Bible verses to memorize. We didn't always stay faithful in our reading and praying together at night, but we make sure to always keep Christ first in our relationship.

Since we were both previously married and had experienced wedding planning, we decided to elope. We started planning a trip to

Savannah, GA, a city we both had wanted to visit. After some research, we found an officiant who performed ceremonies on Tybee Island, right outside of Savannah. We made the arrangements and decided not to tell anyone about our plan. On July 3, 2015, we became Mr. and Mrs.

Since getting married, life has not been perfect. We have disagreements like everyone else, but we try not to explode and make things worse. When a conflict arises in our marriage, one of the first things I do is walk away and pray for Jenn and our situation. That has been my biggest weapon to fight off Satan from getting in between us and our relationship. In August of 2016 we bought a devotional to read together every night. It is Moments Together for Couples by Dennis and Barbara Rainey. Since purchasing this devotional we have completed each day's reading. Some days we may miss one, but we make it up the next day. This devotional has helped us improve our communication, gives us a Bible verse every day, and asks us to pray for something specific. We both agree that it has done wonders in our marriage. We have noticed that if we miss a day or two, tension seems to develop between us and we make it a point to get caught up and focused back on God and our marriage. When I say tensions, I mean we will argue, be annoyed with one another, or get irritated more quickly. So, when we stay committed to the devotional, we notice that our marriage flows smoother because we are so in sync with one another. Nothing comes between us. Having this type of relationship is what we both wanted. We feel so blessed and thankful that God brought us together when He did. I've never been so emotionally, spiritually, and physically attracted to someone. I feel like I am walking on a cloud in my marriage and I feel very undeserving of having such a beautiful wife, but I am reassured in the Word of God, that He takes care of His people and blesses those who are committed to Him.

When my previous marriage ended, I made it a point to start seeing a therapist, so that I could focus on finding my happiness first. I wanted to reacquaint myself with my relationship with God and make sure that He was first in my life and that I looked to Him for everything. When I started to align those things in my life, that is when the blessings started to flow in, and they began with Jenn. In our prayers together at night before we go to bed, we make sure to ask God to help us keep Him at the forefront of our minds, meaning that we are staying committed to Him and that we would grow closer to Him, so that we may grow closer to one another in our marriage.

CHAPTER 13

Fatherhood

"Just as a father has compassion on his children, so the LORD has compassion on those who fear Him," Psalm 103:13

C hristmas Eve 2007, I found out I would be a father for the first time. I mentioned earlier in the book that having a family was a goal of mine for as long as I could remember. The first time I heard, "You are going to be a daddy," I felt excited and a little scared at the same time. The feeling of being scared only lasted for a few moments, it seems, because I knew I would be a good father. To be completely honest though, I wanted to be a great father. Feeling frightened and striving to be the best dad I could be turned out to be a good thing, because it pushed me to dig deeper into reading my Bible and praying daily.

It was a great Christmas present finding out that I was going to be a dad. I wondered if my first born would be a boy or a girl. If it were to be a boy, then I figured a big brother would be there to protect his younger siblings. If it were to be a girl, then I figured I would have a daddy's girl and this brought a huge smile to my face. By the time we were scheduled for the twenty-week ultrasound, my only focus was to have a healthy child that would call me dad. And so, at the ultrasound, we found out we were having a girl.

Madison was born August 23, 2008, and having a daddy's girl is something that is very rewarding. Knowing that you're going to have a child that's going to always want your love and attention means the world to me. We had to go to the hospital for my ex-wife to be induced. She was in the early stages of preeclampsia and it was Madison's due date, August 22. We got there late in the evening and they started giving her meds to induce labor. Her membranes were stripped around 1am and she started having more severe pain. By 3:15am, she was ready to push, and Madison was born at 3:30am. I was excited to cut the umbilical cord and when they asked if I wanted to give her her first bath, I was elated.

I would find out in 2012 that I was going to be a dad for the second time. This time there were no scary feelings, just feelings of excitement and joy. Ava was born on February 9, 2013. Ava's due date was February 14th and I remember my ex-wife drinking castor oil to progress labor along and wanting to have Ava born on her birthday. I do not remember what time Ava was born, but it was cold outside and Ava came into the world healthy. I was also excited about getting to cut her umbilical cord and giving her her first bath. For Madison becoming a big sister, she was excited and really wanted to help out a lot. She would help with whatever she could. I distinctly remember her wanting to help me paint Ava's room. I told her to make sure she was being very careful and not to spill any paint. One of the first things she did was knock over the paint can and spill gray paint all over the carpet in Ava's room. Their relationship is good, and they are usually kind to one another. But just like siblings do, they get on each other's nerves every now and then, and you'll hear them telling each other to stop, until we have to tell them to play separately.

I love being a dad, plain and simple. I wanted to have a family for so long that I really feel like I have won the lottery. It wasn't an easy road getting where I am, happily married with two daughters and a son. In the last chapter I talked, and included Jenn's version, about finding my soul mate after going through a divorce. It was shocking at first when I realized my first marriage was ending because I didn't want to be away from my kids. It felt like a huge part of my world was being taken away from me and I was really upset. But I had the right tools (church and prayer) to help me get through this life transition and still remain a vital part of my daughters' lives. While I wasn't going to be able to have them with me every day, I knew that I would

get them a couple of days each week and we would make special arrangements for holidays and vacations.

God knows all of our days before we are even born and I believe He was bringing me and my girls to Jenn. As awkwardly funny as our first date was, I knew from the moment I saw Jenn that she was the one for me.

First family photo, 2015.

People ask me how I knew this and I like to explain it this way: as I am running towards God in my daily life and I look right and I look left, Jenn is the one I see running beside me.

Jenn got pregnant shortly after we were married and ended up having a miscarriage. Jenn had dealt with miscarriages during her first marriage, but this was the first time I ever dealt with one and I was shell-shocked. It was like a whole new world of things I never expected. The grieving process was in full effect for both of us. I had all these feelings and thoughts that had never occurred to me before. Together, with our undying faith in God and daily prayer, we made it through the miscarriage together. The miscarriage helped us grow as a couple by helping me learn about how she dealt with different situations or different stressors in her life. I was able to see how Jenn overcame obstacles. And all of this reinforced in me that God had blessed my life, and my girls' lives, with the right person for us.

Together, Jenn and I decided to go through the in-vitro process. Jenn's history of miscarriages made trying to conceive naturally, and carry to term, very difficult. I am using Jenn's words to share with you why she has such difficulty carrying a baby to term.

It's probably easier if I take a few moments to explain this part of my life myself, instead of trying to make sure my husband keeps things straight. Miscarriage is not something that society talks about openly. No one warns you it can happen, and no one tells you that it's actually more common than people realize. What isn't common, though, is the genetic disorder I found out I carry back in 2012. You see, while Larry was finding out he was going to have another child, I was finding out why I had just experienced three miscarriages in eleven months. I have what is called a Robertsonian Unbalanced Translocation, located between chromosomes 13 and 14. Without going into all the science behind it, the outcome is that more than half my eggs, once fertilized, would miscarry. After losing my fourth baby in 2015, I was told that I only have approximately a 20% chance of ever carrying a healthy baby to term. This was devastating to hear, but I wanted a child of my own so badly that I was willing to do anything to make it happen (Larry isn't the only one who has stepped outside of God's plan). The next thing we knew, I was being ordered to get bloodwork done several mornings a week, and I was prescribed multiple hormones to inject in myself several times a day.

Jenn took all of the hormone injections as prescribed by the doctor at the fertility clinic. When it was time for the egg retrieval, the doctors were able to get 38 eggs. Of those 38 eggs, we had four healthy embryos to use, and five that could go either way. God, always on time, intervened, and after the shots and the bloodwork, and the egg retrieval, blessed us with a natural conception. We don't believe that the IVF process was wasted, but we were definitely amused at the timing of a healthy, natural pregnancy. We waited until we reached the twelve-week mark before telling anyone that we were expecting. It didn't matter to me whether we had a boy or a girl. I just wanted to have a healthy child because I knew all the pain and heartache that Jenn had been through in the past.

At 16 weeks, we went for our 3-D ultrasound and were told we were having a boy. I was incredibly happy and excited. I have come to realize that having a child is no different whether they are boys or girls. I'm still called to do the same thing. I'm still called father. I'm still called to minister to my family and to be able to raise them up in the way they should live by providing a good foundation of having the Lord in their lives. My children rely on me to teach them about following the Lord. The great reward is what I am able to do in their lives between the time that they're born and the time they go out on their own. But the feeling is also overwhelming. As their dad, am I going to give them the proper foundation to be able to succeed on their own? Am I going to be able to give them everything that they need to succeed in life? Am I going to be able to give them the proper tools to overcome different adversities that they're going to face in their lives? These are the questions I will have to answer to the Lord when I get to heaven. And I know that the Lord is calling me to do these things as a father to my three children.

Levi was born January 14, 2017, 10 days after my birthday, so he is still a Capricorn and I can tell he and I mesh well together on so many levels. Jenn started having contractions late in the evening of Friday the 13th; Levi was due on the 11th, so Jenn was also very uncomfortable and ready to have Levi enter the world. I went to work that day, and Jenn had an appointment with the doctor to find out what the next steps were going to be, so I had been up for a long time. We arrived at the hospital around midnight and then called our doula to meet us there. I was exhausted by the time 3am rolled around and I'm glad we had the doula there. The doula tended to Jenn long enough for me to lie down and close my eyes for an hour and fifteen minutes. Jenn will still make fun of me for sleeping, but I couldn't stay awake any longer. I woke up around 4:30 when I heard a bunch of commotion in the room and Jenn was getting checked. Finally, at 6:57am, Levi arrived after 18 minutes of pushing. I was excited to cut Levi's umbilical cord as well. That is the one job of the dad that I enjoy doing. I know some people may pass out at the sight of blood, but it has never bothered me. The hospital where Levi was born was different than the one where Madison and Ava were born, because their staff actually gave his first bath. While I did not get to do that, I did finally get some more rest whenever Levi was sleeping.

As a father of two girls and a boy, I find it very rewarding being called daddy. It became my mission to be able to teach them and help them learn about Jesus. Teaching about Jesus, His purpose, and that He died for us so we could live eternally with Him is a huge job to take on. And it's not a job for everyone. The last thing I want to be is a deadbeat dad who is nonexistent in my children's lives. This was one of my biggest fears going into fatherhood; I did not want to be a disappointment. The hardest thing in my life has been when I have been told I have disappointed someone. It is something that really eats me alive. It doesn't matter if I hear it from a boss, a friend, family member, my wife, or my children. It is the biggest trigger for sending me into a depressive state because knowing that I've hurt or disappointed somebody really tears me apart. The last thing I ever want to do is be a disappointment to my kids or to let them down. In order to avoid being a disappointment, I turn to the Lord for guidance every day.

I am very proud of my children. Each one has their own distinct personality and it makes being their dad even more gratifying. My oldest daughter, Madison, is like me. She's very level headed and she doesn't like to hurt people. Madison hates to get in trouble because she knows she has disappointed someone or hurt someone's feelings. She gets very upset and cries when she is scolded. My second daughter, Ava, is a very funny, comical, person. She's always on the go and very rambunctious. Ava knows one speed, a million miles an hour, and asks a million questions all the time. My son, Levi Donald (his middle name is in honor of my rack mate who died in the IED explosion), is awesome; he is such a happy baby and full of smiles. He is a morning person like I am and wakes up with the biggest smile to greet whoever is getting him up. Once he is laid on his changing pad, that is when he really comes alive and is smiling. He is a really funny kid with his facial expressions and the things he does as he is eating. Jenn and I always tell each other about the things he does to us while he is eating or playing. I enjoy hearing this from her, since I am gone and at work throughout the majority of the day while also attending classes two nights a week.

What I'm really looking forward to, honestly, is experiencing sports and other extracurricular activities with my kids. It can be dance, art, music, just anything that they are passionate about. My wife and I both love to go to Annapolis, Maryland, and I can't wait to take my son to see the Naval Academy. I will never force my son to join the military but I want him to enjoy watching Navy football and to love Annapolis. I want to start taking Levi to the Army-Navy game when he gets old enough and teach him to be proud of our military. Should he choose not to join the military I'm not going to love him any differently. I'm not going to be disappointed in him. I'm not going to be sad or upset. My hope is that I can instill pride in him for the United States military.

Being a father is something that I love. I want to be able to do it for as long as the Lord allows me to be here and to father the children that He has blessed me with. Aside from Jenn and I praying together, we also pray over Levi every night. When Madison and Ava are here, we make sure to read their Bibles with them individually and to pray with each child before bed. It has been amazing to see the girls slowly grow in Christ and to express their own prayer requests. The girls even take turns saying grace before we eat, even though for Ava it is a simple prayer of, "A B C D E F G, thank you Lord for feeding me." It is important for us to try our best to live out Proverbs 22:6, "Train up a child in the way he should go, and when he is old he will not depart from it."

CHAPTER 14

Jesus Bumps

"When I am in church and feel the Holy Spirit moving, I get Jesus bumps and
that's how I know and feel God's presence with me."

For me, the ultimate reward for accepting God in my life and doing His will has been being able to be a father. There have been plenty of times when I could have turned away from God and lived a worldly life, but each time I have been faced with obstacles, God has found ways to show me He is in charge.

I am often asked, "How do I know that God is with me?" After I became a Christian, after I was saved, I felt like this hole in my heart had been filled with so much love and gratitude. I had this instant feeling that was new and different. This feeling made me able to give myself to others and put others before me. I walked lighter and felt stronger as a man of faith.

I also believe that the word of God is true. Jesus says in the New Testament that once He leaves the earth, He will send His comforter. His comforter is the Holy Spirit. I know the Holy Spirit is here with me, to comfort me, because if I'm feeling convicted about a sin that I have committed, it's a heavy weight bearing down on me and I need to ask for forgiveness. When I'm in church and the Holy Spirit has just filled the room, or if someone is preaching God's word, I get goose bumps. I do not get goose bumps any other time. So instead of calling this phenomenon goose bumps, I call them Jesus bumps. When I am in church and feel the Holy Spirit moving, I get Jesus bumps and that's how I know and feel God's presence with me. I mentioned before that during my accident I felt God with me because of the prayers that had been prayed over me before I had left for Iraq. During those prayers, I had Jesus bumps. Surviving the explosion and making it home from Iraq showed me and made me believe even more that God had a bigger plan for me. He was with me every step of the way and He was going to bring me through all this.

I tell my story so I can help people who are facing their own struggles each day. As I have learned, I want others to know they don't have to live with the difficulties and let the hurdles weigh them down. There are many things that we can do to overcome them and get past what it is that you're facing in your life right now. Sharing my experiences with the Lord is a solid way of life that can make all the difference. I rely on God every day and I want to share four strategies you can use right now that will bring contentment and success to your life.

CHAPTER 15

Faith

"I had those two choices; turn right and go to work or turn left and buy a gun to end my life."

Establishing faith in a higher power is step one in my four-step process. Faith is the belief in a higher power. Believing in something other than yourself is very important because no one walking the earth can possibly know and understand the problems you face on a daily basis. If you are like me, some of my difficulties are issues that I keep inside and use daily prayer and the word of God to help me find resolution. I know that not everyone believes in Jesus Christ and that not everyone is a Christian. For me, my belief in Jesus Christ and my relationship with Christ has been the faith that has gotten me through the rough times and allows me to celebrate the blessings I've been given.

My faith in Jesus Christ has gotten me exactly where I need to be. Through prayer and meditation on the Scripture, I've been able to rely on faith to carry me through my trials and tribulations. I have been able to turn them over to God and trust in Him to carry my burden because sometimes I just can't do it. When it became real that my previous marriage was over, the hardest part for me was not being able to be with my daughters every day. When I let this thought be at the forefront of my day, it really took its toll on me. I couldn't concentrate, I couldn't be efficient at work, and I had trouble sleeping. But out of nowhere I came across the poem, Footprints. The author writes about two sets of footprints in the sand that turn to one set of footprints. These are the times where God carries you through the hard times. After reading the poem, I prayed that God could hear what was in my heart and give me the strength to get through each day. I prayed for His guidance. And I prayed He would watch over my girls as they also were transitioning into a new lifestyle. I slept well that night because I saw two sets of footprints become one as He carried my burden. I woke up having complete trust in knowing my prayers were heard.

If it weren't for my faith in Jesus Christ, I really don't know if I'd still be here today. After my ex-wife left me, I went through a very trying time. I had this gut feeling that she had cheated on me. She swore up and down that she had not. Finally, she came out and told me that she did cheat on me; that she had made out with this guy. And this guy was supposed to be my best friend. He was someone I relied on as a friend and I found out that he tried to sleep with my wife. To make matters worse, I had just spent a week in California visiting him and his wife to just get away from all the stress of our separation. I shared a lot with them about my marriage and how it made me feel like a failure, and I trusted them with my emotions. Both my ex and former best friend have different stories about what exactly happened, but either way she was unfaithful.

I got home from California on a Sunday and had the cheating conversation with my ex-wife. I called out of work on Monday. I just couldn't face the day. On Tuesday, I went to work late. I wasn't really feeling well and I hadn't slept well. I had a migraine. I had all kinds of crazy thoughts in my head. Knowing I would be late for work, I left my house and when I came to the first stop sign, I sat there for a long time. I had two choices running through my head. Turn right and go to work, or turn left and go to the hardware store to buy a gun. Go to work or end my life, because I was so upset that the one friend I was closest to would betray me. By this time, I didn't care too much about what my ex had done; I was moving on. As someone I had briefly served with in Iraq and reconnected with through triathlons, I just couldn't believe that our brotherhood and camaraderie would end up so broken. That was a person I counted on and thought would be there for me at any time. To find out that our friendship was essentially a lie literally almost killed me. However, I couldn't get the image of my daughters out of my head. I kept seeing them being left in this world without Dad. I thought about statistics showing that children who have a parent who committed suicide are more likely to commit suicide. I knew right then and there I was going to go to work. I chose work, I chose life, I chose my kids, and I chose to never speak to that friend again.

While the image of my kids initially got me through that moment, it's really my relationship with Christ that ultimately pulled me through. He put the image of my daughters in my head. He reminded me on that day, and many times before and after, that I don't want to lose my relationship with Him. I didn't want to take anything away from God as He's working through my life so that I'm able to tell my story and help others overcome barriers. My relationship with and my faith in Jesus Christ kept me from ending my own life a long time ago. I felt as if I was always dealing with demons. I still deal with demons and emotions that no person should ever have to deal with. As someone who served in the military that's what we volunteered for. We know going in that we will see and do things most people in this world will never see or do. For me, it was my faith in Jesus Christ that helps me deal with my demons from what I saw and did while at war. Through His love for me, I found new purpose and meaning for my life and my desire to live. And because of that faith, I want to be able to do God's work and use my story to help people.

When I look back now, I cannot fathom how I ever considered ending my life. My kids need me here on this earth more than I feel like I need to not be on this earth. As I said before, my role as a dad is my number one call to ministry. I need to be able to be here for my kids. I need to teach them how to succeed in life and give them the tools they need to do so. And if I'm not here then I can't do it. I don't really want someone else raising my kids for me when I'm fully capable of being here to show them who I am and that my faith in Christ has carried me to where I am today. I want to show my children that by relying on Christ and using the tools that The Bible has given us to live our lives, they can overcome anything. In order to overcome things, you have to have faith in a higher power. Having faith in Buddha, Mohammed, Christ, or some other higher being is the most important thing in life to be able to help you move forward.

CHAPTER 16

Support

"Your support system may not understand the reasons behind your goals, but they have your back unconditionally."

The second step to living your life and overcoming obstacles thrown in front of you is to create a great support system. When your support system understands your goals, they become your cheerleaders on each step of your journey. Even when you stumble, they are there to help pick you back up. Your support system may not understand the reasons behind your goals, but they have your back unconditionally. These are the people you want in your life who enhance your energy instead of draining you to the point of exhaustion. The people you include can be family and or friends of any age and background. The hardest part with creating your support system is determining who in your life is genuine and who is just providing lip service and using you for their own gain. Honestly, weeding out your support system can take several attempts and you should be prepared for mistakes along the way.

I have made my share of mistakes when it comes to those I considered my strongest supporters. My ex-wife was not supportive in the ways I needed her to be. For example, I had various opportunities for jobs once I retired from the Navy that would have made things much better for our family, but her support just wasn't there. I was going to school but I was also struggling to really figure out what it was that I wanted to do. My marriage with her was all about doing everything for the kids. And that isn't a bad thing. I already mentioned that being a father is my gift from God. However, in order to be the dad I needed to be for my children, two daughters at that time, I needed to have the opportunity to figure out my calling for my next job. It was hard. After all, a few years earlier I thought my calling was the Navy for 20 years. Losing that calling was not a choice I made. It was decided for me that day I became a lone survivor. I needed time and patience. I needed a support system. It wouldn't be until I married Jenn that I would have the support I needed to go to nursing school and answer the call to help others.

There was one area in my life where my ex-wife provided unconditional support, and it was sports. She liked it when I was accomplishing things through athletics. Knowing I had her encouragement in this arena, I really overcompensated when it came to sports. I would eventually put so much pressure on my body that it has become physically impossible to participate in the events that are my favorites. But after recovering from the IED explosion, I saw athletics as a new way to find contentment in life.

CHAPTER 17

The Making Of An Ironman

"Larry Perry, you are an Ironman."

After watching the Ironman World Championships in Kona, Hawaii, on television, I wanted to be an Ironman. I wanted to do it for myself, and I wanted to do it for Madison. I wanted to hear, "Larry Perry, You Are An Ironman!" Besides becoming addicted to the Ironman and training for it, I just wanted to prove to people that I am an injured service member who has overcome thirty surgeries and here I am, a full blown Ironman. That means I completed a 2.4 mile swim, a 112 mile bike ride, and a 26.2 mile marathon for a total of 140.6 miles all in one day, without a break.

When I started triathlon training, I was still married to my previous wife and my second daughter had not yet been born. My support system was in place with my ex and my four-year old daughter. For Christmas, 2009, I bought my first bicycle and I made the commitment to myself to become an Ironman. By June 2010, I had completed my first mini triathlon, which consisted of a quarter-mile swim, ten-mile bike ride, and a two-mile run. I was proud of my finish and my ex-wife was proud of how fit I was becoming.

After completing that triathlon, I was hooked. Triathlon is a totally different kind of sport. While each triathlon is a competition, the level of support is amazing. Every other athlete competing is cheering for you as well. If there's someone left out on the course, no one is going to let you cross the finish line by yourself. Tri-athletes will be there to cheer you on and walk beside you to the finish line. There is a lot of camaraderie out there and it was great for me to add more people to my support system. At this time in my life, I missed being in the military. I missed serving with my brothers in the Marines that I had been stationed with. Having that camaraderie and the family type of environment while competing in triathlons was something that I was longing for and that I really needed. I completed my first Half Ironman race on September 11, 2011, the ten-year anniversary of 9/11, at Cedar Point amusement park in Ohio. The feeling I had when I crossed the finish line was amazing. It is an addiction, really, and I got hooked on that feeling of accomplishment.

At the end of 2010, I knew I needed to ramp up my game. I started looking for a coach because I didn't really know how to train myself to complete an entire 140.6 -mile triathlon. I picked up a magazine, and there was an article about the Naval Academy Triathlon Team and how they had won back-to-back championships. I liked what I saw in their coach. His name was Billy Edwards and he was also a professional triathlete. He was a Naval Academy graduate and I knew I needed to reach out to this guy. I found his email and asked him what it would take to get him to train me. Together we devised a plan and he would send me workouts to do online so that I could build up my aerobic and anaerobic capacity. Billy was my coach for a long time, helping me complete my Ironman, and then working with me on marathons. He played a huge roll in my support system and even today, Coach Billy still has my back.

In November 2011, I went to Ironman Florida to Volunteer and sign up for the race the following year. That is the best way to get your ticket to the race. Florida is one of the Ironman's that sells out quickly. They usually sell out within a few hours after being open to the public, but if you go down and volunteer at the race, you can stand in line to sign up for the next year and get a guaranteed slot. While volunteering, I received bikes from people coming in off the bike course. I would take their bike from them and someone would replace it on the rack for them. This was such a great experience and I enjoyed cheering on all the athletes. So I paid my $600 registration fee and told myself there was no backing out. It cost entirely too much money for me to change my mind.

Following the registration, Billy and I started to ramp up my training program. I had a year to get myself into shape and to be ready to complete the Ironman. I had no idea the toll it would put on my mind, body, and soul, but it was worth it. I think I may have slacked off in my training a bit during the winter holiday season, but I made sure to do as much training as I could during those months. That included running outside, riding my bike inside on the trainer or outside on the road when it was clear of salt and the weather was nice. If it was 50 degrees or above, I was outside riding. I also did a lot of my work that winter in the pool. With my left elbow being flail, I wanted to make sure that my freestyle swim stroke was ready to go, and that I was going to do well in the water on the 2.4 mile swim. Up to that point, I am not even sure if I had done a long swim, but I was willing to do whatever I had to do to get myself ready for that grueling swim.

During my training in 2012, I started to have issues with my back while I was riding my bike. I could ride for 80 miles in the aerodynamic position and then I would have to start sitting up because my back was in so much pain. After having X-Rays and an MRI done, my doctor informed me that I had a herniated disc in L5. That was a little bit of a crushing blow to my training, but I pushed through it and realized that if I had to sit up for the last 30 or so miles and switch from sitting up to the aerodynamic position, then that is what I would do during the race. With the herniated L5 came muscle spasms, so I had to make sure that when my back started to flare up, that I was doing what I could to prevent the muscle spasms from occurring, in order to get through the run. Since I had lost so much weight during my training, the muscle spasms were not as bad as they are today, but I could feel my back starting to flare up during long rides.

As I just stated above, I had lost so much weight during this training, that my knees were holding up pretty well during all of my runs. One of the things we implemented in the Ironman training was that I would try to run for 30 minutes, take a 1 minute walking break, and then run for another 30 minutes and so on. That worked well during training and going into the race I felt great about our game plan. I was shooting for a goal of 12 hours for the race, but as usual, things never turn out as I expect.

Since the Ironman was such an all-around intense experience, from my training regimen to the increase in my daily calorie intake, to the actual race day, I want to take you through the days leading up to the race and the through the race day itself as if you had been there with me.

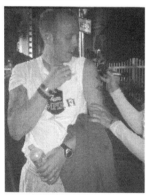

Getting my markings.

It's four days before the race. We're supposed to leave tomorrow, October 31, 2012. A weather alert came across the news that a hurricane is approaching Maryland through the Chesapeake Bay, so it's imperative that we leave tonight. We have to rush to pack the car and at this point we're just hoping that we aren't forgetting anything, because we're now heading out tonight. We need to leave quickly because they are about to shut down the bridges due to high wind restrictions. By 1pm we are pulling out of the driveway and I'm officially on my way to the Ironman race. Thankfully we've made it out of Maryland in time before the storm caused all sorts of issues, and we plan to stop in South Carolina to sleep for the night.

Day Two: We've been in the car for a total of 19 hours and I'm excited to finally be in Panama City, but anxiety is now creeping in because in three short days I will be competing in the longest race of

my life. I know there are several things to do in order to get prepared for Saturday, so I started checking things off my list by starting off with a run. I'm running through the streets of Panama City and I'm seeing other competitors as I check out part of the course. Seeing the course is making me realize just how long of a day I'm going to have ahead of me. After 45 minutes of running, I'm back at our condo where it's time to unpack and unwind and figure out where we're going to go for dinner.

Hanging out with Madison before the race.

Day Three: I'm now extremely anxious as I wait for my bike to arrive. My in-laws are bringing it in their car and they still haven't made it to Panama City. I need to get to the airport though, so I can't worry about my bike for long. Now heading to pick up Coach Billy from Northwest Florida Beaches International Airport, I'm feeling excited again because I know he will have some solid advice on how I can remain focused for the rest of today and tomorrow before I finally wake up on race day, Saturday. As we drive 30 minutes from the airport to the car, Billy is asking me questions about the training I've done since arriving. He's telling me to relax but that's not the easiest thing for me to do right now.

Back at the condo with Billy, we decide to go for a swim in the Gulf of Mexico. We're not talking in the water, we're just swimming and I'm focused on keeping my muscles loose and my body moving. I know this is important because I don't want to tense up and have my body shut down during the race in a couple of days. We've been swimming approximately 20 minutes and Billy tells me that I'm done. We go back into the condo and I'm right back to waiting on my bike. I'm sitting around the condo just trying to relax and finally my in-laws arrive with my bike. I can't help them unload their car fast enough because I'm so pumped to get my bike put together, lubed, and ready to ride. I'm finally riding my bike and riding for about 45 minutes. Back at the condo, it's time to get ready for dinner. This is the night where it's most important for me to get a good night's sleep because I know tomorrow night I will be entirely too anxious and excited to get much rest. It's 10:00 PM and I'm in bed.

Day Four: I woke up very refreshed and very thankful for a good night's rest. Today I have to prepare my gear bags and my bike so that I can turn them in to the race volunteers before dinner. I decide to go out and train first, so I'm on my bike for 20 minutes and then I'll run for 15. I'm back in the condo and finally getting my bags together. I'm grateful that Billy is here to help me because he's a professional triathlete and keeps giving me great tips and tricks for how to get my bags together. I have three bags in front of me; one for my transition from the swim to the bike, one for the transition from the bike to the run, and another one for the halfway point of the run. In the first bag is my bike

Coming out of the water.

outfit, two sandwiches, five energy gels, bike shoes, compression socks, and a towel. Bag two contains a pair of compression socks, running shoes, my tri-suit, running belt with four bottles of Gatorade, more energy gels, a hat and sunglasses. Over in bag three is an extra pair of compression socks, a hat, another pair of running shoes, and more energy gels. With all three bags ready to go, I take them, along with my bike, to the race volunteers and we head to the athlete's dinner hosted by the Ironman race directors. Dinner was a pasta buffet for carb loading. After dinner we make our way to the after party on the beach and I'm meeting and socializing with professional triathletes who will be competing with me tomorrow. I'm in shock because Coach Billy is introducing me to all of these men and women because he happens to know them personally and trains with them. I know I don't want to be here long, even though it's been awesome talking to these pros, but I need to get back to the condo and get some sleep. Tomorrow is a big day.

Day Five: It's now race day and I am very anxious. It's 4:00 AM and I'm tired and trying to make sure that I can grab breakfast. After eating two eggs and toast with both water and chocolate milk to drink, I get dressed. I put on a pair of swim jammers (long, tight swim shorts) to wear under my wet suit. The race is set to start at 7:00 AM. As we leave the condo, I'm still anxious but I'm also ready to just get into the water and start the race.

It's 6:15 AM and we're on the beach. The beach is very crowded full of spectators and family members there to cheer everyone on. The professional triathletes start their race ten minutes before everyone else. After they

Running towards my bike.

start, everyone else can get in the water and warm up a little bit. I get in the water and get in some decent strokes, and made sure I was wet and warmed up. Everyone is looking at their watches. I know it's 7:00 AM because the gun finally goes off and the race has begun. The first lap of the swim (it is a two lap swim course) is difficult for the first 15 minutes until I've created enough of a gap to not hit anyone else or get hit by another swimmer's hands or feet. That is the roughest part of the race, but probably the most fun too. After the first lap, I'm feeling really good, but one of the things that ticks me off is that all of these spectators on the beach do not allow you the room to get out of the water and run along the beach back to the starting point of the course. When we (the swimmers) get out of the water to where we re-enter the water, there is about 200-400 feet of space and the spectators close in, making it difficult to get through quickly. There is not a rule anywhere stating you have to stay in the water, so the most energy efficient way to approach this is to get out of the water and run along the sand to the starting area to start lap two. I am not running through the water to exert all of my energy, so I fight my way through the crowd. I start lap two and it is much smoother because there are not 2500 people getting in the water at the same time. I make it through the checkpoint after the swim in 1:18:13 and I am so happy with my time. While training I was doing my workouts in about 90-100 minutes swimming the same distance. I know in the pool I was taking breaks between sets, so my goal was to swim in under 90 minutes. Finishing in the time I did feels awesome.

Starting my run.

I run out of the water, see my family and Billy, and the volunteers strip my wetsuit off of me. (If you ever had to take off a wetsuit in a race, then you know this is not an easy task.) The volunteers made me sit on my butt and they just rip it off of my legs which is great, and then I carry it with me after that. I run into the changing area and put on some riding shorts with the thick butt because 112 miles will be grueling. I have peanut butter and jelly (PB&J) sandwiches in my clothes already packed and ready to go. I also have GU energy gels with me, so that I have calories for my ride. On my bike, I have Gatorade and other nutrition drinks to keep my calorie intake up while riding. I get on my bike and have to run it out to the start area, my whole transition feels to be around 7 minutes. I'm off onto the bike ride and I feel great. The humidity is a little higher than expected, so I make sure to try to save myself and my legs for the run by cruising at a pretty easy pace and making sure that I keep up with my training plan. On the bike my training plan was to ride smooth, and make sure that every 30 minutes I am putting calories in my system. I take either a gel or PB&J every 30 minutes while sipping Gatorade as I need it throughout the ride. This plan is working well, but as fate would have it, at about mile 75, my back flares up. I have to start sitting up more after being in the aerodynamic position for these first 75 miles. I am okay with this because I want to be able to save my legs for the run anyway. I get through the bike leg with no other issues and I complete this in 5:47:08. I averaged 19.4 mph overall for the bike. I feel happy with that as my goal was to try to average 20 mph. I knew if my back played a factor, it would be tough to get the 20 mph the entire length of the bike ride.

I get off the bike, run in to change, and I feel my stomach starting to act up. I don't feel good, like I need to throw up, and my legs feel really heavy. I made sure I wore compression socks on the ride so that the blood flow was good in my legs on the bike course. This transition lasts about 7-10 minutes. I'm really feeling sick but I'm pushing through to get myself together and focusing on getting my compression socks on properly.

I head out on the run. I've been running maybe 2 miles and I have to start walking. Billy is now beside me yelling at me the entire way, telling me to pick up my game. He's trying to motivate me, but I'm 7 hours and 5 minutes into the race and I know I have about 10 hours to finish. I know it won't take me that long to walk a full marathon, so

I'm on coasting mode. I have plenty of time to finish, but I cannot get my legs to fire and all I keep telling Billy is that I want to throw up. He tells me no, you have to keep your calories in you and you need to keep pushing, come on. This first leg of the 2 loop run is just brutal. There is a whole lot of walking and not a lot of running. I run where I can, but when I get around to the second loop and see Madison and other family members there to support me, a fire

Seeing Madison during my run of the IronMan, 2012.

finally ignites in me and I am able to get my legs to start running more. My breaks aren't as long now. Billy is still out here on the second loop with me. It is so awesome having this motivation and support from Billy. Seeing Madison at the beginning of this loop definitely brought a smile to my face so now I'm really excited to get to the finish line and see her again. The run has been the longest and worst leg of the entire race. I finish the run in 7:05:06 for a total race time of 14:27:21. I finally hear the words I've been longing to hear, "Larry Perry, you are an Ironman."

In the midst of my excitement at the finish line, I had a breakdown and immediately thought about Donald. It had been 6 years and 8 days since our accident. I was emotional because of all the hard work I put into my training and thinking about the ways I had overcome the adversity and injuries I faced to get me where I was at that exact moment in time. My ex-wife was there to put the Finisher's Medal around my neck and she was very excited and proud. Getting to see Madison and having her jump up and down with excitement and then jump into my arms when I finished was emotional as well. Having Billy there, pushing me to the finish line was fantastic. I was finally an Ironman and I was really proud of that accomplishment. I had not only proven the doctors wrong who told me I may never walk again, but I went above and beyond to prove to myself that I could do anything I set my mind to.

CHAPTER 18

Support That Sustains

"The best way to show my children what true love looks like is through my life with Jenn."

I became an Ironman in 2012 and ran my last marathon in 2013 in Virginia Beach. That was the last time I physically have been able to train for those types of sports. At the end of the Shamrock Marathon in Virginia Beach, I found out my knees were shot. I talked about all the trauma both knees sustained in the explosion and after years of training and competing, my knees could no longer support that type of regimen.

When I finally gave in to the pain and realized that my days of triathlon and marathon training were over, I decided to try CrossFit. I wanted to stay active, and I wanted to maintain an athletic support system. Two of my closest friends were heavily involved in their local CrossFit gym, and my ex-wife was highly motivated to start her own CrossFit journey. She tried it for the first time with our friends, and excitedly suggested I give it a try. As with all things I set my mind to do, I gave CrossFit 110% but at the end of the day, or in this case a year, I found that my body wasn't able to handle the movements needed for CrossFit. Because of my flail elbow, I had absolutely no stability in my left arm. I would raise my arm up in the air and my elbow would fall all over the place. Basically, my left arm was kind of along for the ride and my right arm was doing the majority of the work. Then I realized my knees weren't made for CrossFit either. They started swelling up and any attempt to lift weights or do squats resulted in my knees feeling like they were going to give out in the middle of the exercise. They were also very painful the next day.

I really wanted to make CrossFit work for both my body and my mind. The camaraderie is very similar to triathlons and I really like that atmosphere. I also thrive when I'm feeling supported by those around me. But it wasn't the same "high" for me as marathons or triathlons were, and I found myself stepping away. Exercise does mean enduring some levels of pain; that I know. But after suffering the injuries I got in Iraq, the pain as a result of working out was very depressing for me. My time in CrossFit, plus moving to different gyms based on where we were living, didn't add much to my support system. And when I needed my ex to really step up and understand what was happening with my body and my mental status because I couldn't exercise, she just wasn't there. That was the beginning of the downward spiral that would end our marriage.

My youngest daughter, Ava, was born February 2013. We were also celebrating our 5th wedding anniversary and my ex was turning twenty-five years old. Two months after Ava was born, my ex said to me that she was not sexually attracted to me anymore because of my weight. I knew that I wasn't as toned as I was when I was training for triathlons, and that I was still searching for the right job, but her comment hit me like a ton of bricks. I lost all respect for her. I lost my trust in her and I was in a downward spiral of depression. I was still me; a little heavier, but I was still the same guy.

When I'm depressed, I spend money impulsively and I binge eat for comfort. What she said to me didn't help matters with my weight and I started making poor decisions. I ran up our credit cards and put us in a spot of debt because of that hurtful thing she said. I have no idea why I decided to stay with her and try to work through things.

For most people, when they are told this, they just shut down and walk away. But I stayed because I really yearned for the family dynamic. I really just wanted to be in my kids' lives all the time. And I knew that no matter what state I was living in, Pennsylvania or Maryland, more than likely I wasn't going to get custody of my daughters full time. I stayed. Shell shocked and hurt by her statement, I stayed. She left July 4th, 2014, and she said that she just wasn't happy. At that point in my life, my support system consisted of my two daughters and a few friends. I felt like my ex-wife bailed out on me when I gained weight. She exited my support system way before she physically walked out the door.

I mentioned earlier that there would be some trial and error when it comes to finding the right people for your support system. It's no different for me. This experience in my previous marriage led me to a lot of self-discovery though psychotherapy. I learned about myself and who I am. I learned to identify the things in my life that I need and want. There's a book by Gary Chapman called The Five Love Languages and I know that my primary love language is "words of affirmation". Through therapy, I learned who I wanted to be in my relationship with Christ, as well as what I was yearning for in my next partner.

As I look back on things now, I know, without a doubt, that I was never truly in love. My choice to stay with her was for the sake of our kids because I wanted to be a prominent figure in their lives. She wasn't happy. I really wasn't happy. I was miserable. Looking back, I'm thankful that she came to me when she did to end our marriage, rather than dragging out a life of unhappiness.

Today, my ex-wife and I have a relationship that is focused on the kids. There's no spite, and I'm grateful that neither one of us are in a situation where we are miserable. Our daughters deserve to see what love and happiness really look like, even if it is between two homes. She is now back in my support system, but playing a different role. When it comes to co-parenting, we experience our share of struggles, but at the end of the day we always come together to do what is best for our kids. We don't make the kids choose who to sit with at school events or extra-curricular activities because we all sit together, usually to the amusement of others. Our version of normal is completely different from what many experience with blended families. By no means do we have it all figured out, but I'm proud of the steps we have taken over the last few years to get to this point. I think that where we failed each other as spouses, we make up for in parenting. We always find a way to support the custody schedule the other needs and work hard to make sure that our daughters' lives flow as seamlessly as possible.

The best way to show my children what true love looks like is through my life with Jenn. Meeting and marrying Jenn has been such a blessing for me. I knew God was front and center of my support system when He brought us together. My relationship with her is on such a totally different level than I could have expected any relationship to be. Jenn is the most supportive person I've ever met. She supports my goals, my dreams, and aspirations. However, Jenn doesn't support everything that comes out of my mouth. She stands firm in her convictions and tries to help guide me to make the best choices for me and for our family. If she completely supported every little thing I say, then we'd be living a very reckless life. Fortunately, Jenn's support helps to keep me grounded, and she always finds a way to help me narrow down what it is that I'm wanting to do. When we were living in Maryland, she jumped right on board with us moving and starting a life together just outside of DC because of my job. Jenn was standing right next to me when I realized being a federal employee, working in Washington, D. C. wasn't the right "fit" for me. She could see my depression coming back after my ex-wife took the girls and moved to Lancaster, Pennsylvania. The drive from Columbia, Maryland to Lancaster, Pennsylvania was 95 miles one way. Jenn could see the effects this was having on my well-being and the well-being of our blended family. Together, we decided the best choice for us would be to move to Pennsylvania so we could be closer to the girls. This is my support system in action.

Jenn gets along with my ex-wife. They were friends years before my ex and I got married. For that I am grateful, because it has honestly helped each of us as we have transitioned into a blended family. Their friendliness with one another has helped all of us grow our relationships with the kids in every aspect. We are a great team of parents.

God created, in His time, the support systems for both Jenn and me. There are times I wish it had happened sooner and I hadn't been hurt during my previous marriage, but all things happen for a reason. He definitely had a plan for Jenn and me and it is truly amazing. I feel like I know true spiritual love. God does everything for a reason and He was building me into the person He wanted me to be. And then He brought me Jenn; I have never been in a relationship like this before. I'm so grateful and so blessed to have Jenn in my life as my wife, mother of our son, and bonus mom to my daughters.

When I walk through the door at the end of the day, I smile with a full heart not just because of my children, but also because I have a supportive wife. Somebody who is helping me to achieve my goals and to live my dream. Jenn is the reason I am able to have a family and able to go to nursing school. This is what it's all about. There is nothing that can come between Jenn and me because I'm just so in love with her and we both are in love with God. For us to be on the same page, running the same race at the same speed, makes every day so much easier than it has been in the past. As I said in Step One, I'm really glad that I listened to the Holy Spirit that day and drove to work. Having Jenn as my support system and having kids to come home to every day, is an affirmation that God had His hand on me and made living each day worth it. This is what God had in store for me. It's a blessing to be here at this stage of my life. God's blessing of Jenn and three beautiful children will keep me going until the day I die. Whether I die from old age or something else takes me sooner, I will continue to live on and press forward. Whether we add more children to our family or we remain a family of five, it's just a blessing to have her beside me in my journey. I am the luckiest man alive because my support system consists of God, Jenn, and my children.

CHAPTER 19

Forgiveness

"If we can't forgive the people that have wronged us and have hurt us in the past, then why should Christ continue to forgive us every day for the sins we commit?"

The third step necessary to moving forward in life is forgiveness. To learn how God, or faith in a higher being, can guide us to forgiveness takes some time at first. Daily prayer and reading my Bible, along with going to therapy for depression after my previous marriage ended, gave me the tools I would need to make forgiveness an easy thing to do. In Matthew 6:9-13, Jesus is going through the Lord's Prayer and says, "forgive us our debt as we forgive our debtors." If we can't forgive those that hurt us then why should Christ forgive us? That's how I look at forgiveness. If we can't forgive the people that have wronged us and who have hurt us in the past, then why should Christ continue to forgive us every day for the sins we commit? He paid the ultimate sacrifice on Calvary's Tree when He was nailed to the cross and died for us for the forgiveness of sins and so we would be able to spend eternity with Him. He died lovingly and willingly for the entire world. All we have to do is ask Him to forgive us. And that's why I said it's kind of easy for me to forgive.

The first thing I had to do for myself during my recovery was forgive myself for volunteering to go back to Iraq right after I finished a deployment. I blame myself a little bit for what happened because my actions basically allowed this to happen. In Hebrews chapter 12 God says that He chastises those He loves. For me, that's what it's about. I was out of line. I was not living my life according to God's word and His plan for my life. He had to humble me and get my attention. God basically took me out to the woodshed and gave me the beating that I needed for my terrible actions. So I had to forgive myself a little bit because I was the majority of the problem by putting myself in that situation. I had to forgive myself in order to move forward in life and live God's will for me.

Believe it or not, I had to forgive the Iraqis who were hiding out in the bushes under the palm trees and detonated that bomb. I hope that one day this book will land in the arms of one of them who did this to me. I want them to see that I have forgiven them and moved on with my life. Actually, if I were to meet one of them, I know in my heart that I would walk up to him, give him a hug, and thank him for where I am today. If it weren't for those who detonated the bomb that day, I would have many "what if's." I might not have a story to tell, I might not have this powerful testimony to share, I might not be able to be the man God intended. But I had to learn that we don't need to live in "what if's," and I worked very hard to forgive them and move on with my life.

Let's suppose, for a second, I hadn't been able to forgive and step forward into happiness. Holding onto anger and bitterness against the Iraqis who blew me up would have led to extreme depression and just being a miserable soul. I would be very hostile towards people from that part of the world. The anger and bitterness would consume me and it would impact my ability to be a great husband and father. Why, you ask? Because I would be angry all the time and reliving the accident, day in and day out. God helped me to see that by following His plan I would be too busy sharing my testimony to have time to focus on anger and bitterness.

I've also learned to forgive my mom for what she said to me before I left for boot camp. She told me that she thought I would quit boot camp like I quit everything else in my life. It was hurtful and disappointing to hear those words come from my own mother's mouth, but in the end, it's what pushed me to get through boot camp. That's not the only thing my mom has said to me over the years that has been hurtful. While she was amazing at supporting me during my immediate recovery, we have since become estranged. We can't seem to find a common ground on an appropriate way to talk and behave around my kids. However, despite her words and actions, I forgive her, and I love her from a distance.

Forgiveness doesn't require an apology from the person who hurt you, and that's something I'll probably never get from my mom, but it doesn't matter. Forgiveness is something you feel within yourself, and something you do for yourself to move forward, not necessarily for the other person. There's a song by Matthew West called Forgiveness. This is one of my favorite songs because it talks about the process of forgiveness and that the person who is set free by forgiveness is you. This is so true for me. I've never been more free because I have forgiven those who have wronged or hurt me in some way.

Using what I have learned about forgiveness and the role it plays in moving forward, I had to forgive my ex-wife for the hurtful words that she spoke about my weight and for being unfaithful. Deciding to work with a therapist on this played a big part in my healing process, and set the stage for my new life moving forward. Finding myself and forgiving her has allowed us to work together to become a great co-parenting team.

If there is someone in your life that needs to be forgiven, don't waste another minute. It will set you free, it will set them free, and it has the power to breathe new life into your relationship. You can't control whether or not you'll hear "I'm sorry" but you can control whether or not you'll say "I forgive you."

CHAPTER 20

Laugh

"It was so memorable and I laughed so hard that, for a brief moment, I forgot how much pain I was in."

Where would I be if I couldn't laugh every day? I would be living in misery somewhere. You have heard the saying that "laughter is the best medicine," and I can tell you that is the absolute truth. The fourth step is laughter. After having thirty surgeries and all the other medical issues associated with the explosion, there is no way I would have healed as fast as I did if I wasn't laughing. Laughter kept me from feeling sorry for myself and soaking up pity and sympathy from others.

Reaching the point where I could tell jokes to make others laugh, as well as feeling confident enough in my own day-to-day struggles to laugh at myself, wasn't an easy road after the explosion in Iraq. Fortunately, I have always had a good sense of humor, so even if I wanted to keep a sour face while in the hospital, when stuff was funny, I laughed. It is always easier to laugh when you have family and friends around. So when I got to Bethesda and I started to have visits from people I knew, I would laugh a lot when we would tell stories. There are a few stories I vaguely remember from the hospital that made me laugh. I remember going into one of my last surgeries and being given the feel good juice before I went to sleep for the surgery. I remember them telling me to talk, so I started saying do you want me to tell you a funny story and the next thing I knew, I was out. That just made me laugh because here I was trying to make other people laugh and I just fell asleep. Another thing I did with the doctors who were doing my final arm surgery, where they took out the rod and screws that were in my left elbow and removed the left elbow, was to set up the head doctor who was not in the room with us at the time. My favorite orthopedic surgeon, Dr. M. T. Newman, and I set up the head surgeon, Dr. Anderson. Dr. Newman decided we would play a joke on Dr. Anderson because Dr. Anderson was a little anal retentive, making sure everything was done to a T (which is probably the best way to be as a surgeon). He asked Dr. Newman a few times if he got everything out of my arm and Dr. Newman assured him he had. Dr. Anderson asked to see the x-rays showing everything was out of the arm and Dr. Newman put the rod and screws on top of the bandage after they had taken everything out and took the x-rays for Dr. Anderson to see. Dr. Anderson came flying down to the OR and then saw that it was a set-up and he was not too happy about it. But Dr. Newman and I just laughed and laughed about it.

My mom and dad knew I was a big fan of comedian Ralphie May since he appeared on Last Comic Standing, and my mom decided to reach out to him while he was in Washington, D.C. for a gig. She asked if he would come and visit with me in the hospital and if we could come to one of his shows. Believe it or not, he came to the hospital to meet me. While he was there he asked if I was able to leave the hospital to come to his show, and the hospital granted permission. I hung out backstage in my wheelchair and spent the night laughing my butt off. Being able to go backstage was definitely one of the coolest times I have ever had. I also got to see his wife, Lahna Turner, do her standup comedy that same night. It was so memorable and I laughed so hard that for a brief moment, I forgot how much pain I was in. My favorite jokes of Ralphie's are when he makes fun of himself. Someone who can make fun of themselves and make other people laugh doing it is great comedy to me. I make fun of myself all the time, but Ralphie being a big guy like he is, talks about his gastric bypass surgery and how he lost 150 pounds after having it done. He goes on to say that he lost the weight of a whole person, but how he is still fat. That joke can make me laugh for hours just hearing him tell it.

I try to laugh every day whether it is laughing with others or laughing at myself. I probably laugh at myself more than I laugh at anybody else or at something anybody else says. I am such a happy person these days that I just want to laugh. Jenn and I laugh at each other all the time. I am a very random person and just come up with things out of nowhere, so when I come up with one of these things, I can always expect the same response out of her, "I just can't deal with you right now." It's not a funny sentence but the way she says it, and the reasons why just always seem to crack me up.

Levi, even as a baby, makes me laugh every day. His smile just lights up the room but he seems to do it at what can be inconvenient times, like in the middle of drinking his bottle. Next thing you know, formula is coming out of his mouth because he's smiling instead of swallowing, then he starts giggling and I do, too. He currently grabs at everything, including my beard. When he does, I rub my beard against his hand and he will just light up with this big smile and it makes me laugh. Making Levi laugh also makes me laugh. He is very ticklish around his neck, so I blow raspberries on his neck and get him laughing. He is also ticklish on his inner thighs and his belly. I blow a lot of raspberries on his belly and he starts his uncontrollable deep belly laugh. He doesn't know it yet, but his laugh and our shared laughs make any bad days 100% better.

My daughters can also make me laugh, especially Ava, because of her age. Without telling a story that will embarrass her when she's older, it was hilarious to hear about her mom teaching her about her anatomy. Just thinking about it makes me laugh right now, but I know she'll be pretty upset with me when she's older if I were to tell the full story behind the reasons she learned everything so young. Ava also comes up with the most random stuff. For example, Madison was enrolled in a summer camp called Camp Summer Sunshine. Somehow, this prompted Ava to start calling her days with Jenn "Camp Jenny Sunshine". It was completely out of the blue and for the entire summer she would talk about going on field trips with Camp Jenny Sunshine. Madison is older but followed suit, and didn't understand why they don't have camp t-shirts or go on behind the scenes tours at the local dairy farms when they go out for ice cream.

As you can tell, my kids provide me with endless things to laugh about. If laughter doesn't come easy for you, put it on your daily to-do list and purposefully make an effort to laugh every day. Find a YouTube clip of your favorite comedian, download your favorite comedy, call up a friend and talk about that time something hilarious happened. Just laugh. Keep that smile on your face and keep on pushing forward towards your goal.

CHAPTER 21

Injury to Ironman

"I can do all things through Christ who strengthens me" Philippians 4:13

After my accident and throughout my recovery, my biggest "what if" moment was, what if this never happened to me, where would I be? Before my accident, I wanted to make a career out of the Navy and try to stay in for at least 20 years. I also wanted to leave Iraq, return to Hawaii, take my advancement exam, and go right back to Iraq. I wanted to join the special warfare combatant-craft crewmen (the SWCC forces). These guys drive the high-speed boats that take SEALS into land and they have high-powered machine guns mounted in the boats. That was what I wanted to do. I have always loved the water and boats. But God had other plans.

By accepting God's will and letting go of trying to control everything in my life, I started to see quite clearly the things I did not want to miss in life. I wanted to be present and an active participant in being a dad, and I wanted to have a partner in life who put God first in our marriage and family.

There are other things on my to-do list, too. I want to travel to Europe. I want to fly upside down in a plane, preferably with the Blue

Angels one time I want to sky dive, bungee jump, go 200 mph in either a car or on a motorcycle, and I really want to do this human water catapult thing. I am a huge adrenaline junky, so anything that gets my adrenaline pumping are things I want to check off my bucket list.

I am not big on having regrets in my life because everything has led me to where I am today. Everything happened for a reason and God had a plan for it all to bring me here. Yes, I wish I would have made better choices in my relationship with Him as far as doing things I think that He called me to do. Maybe I wouldn't have been blown up or even in the military, but I cannot tell you how rewarding this experience has been for me and what all it has taught me. I have learned humility, how to really let Jesus be Lord of my life and running all my decisions by Him first. I have also learned about agape love and what it truly means to love people for who they are.

I have reached the point in my life that when I think back to the accident, I don't really have any questions. I just thank God that I am alive. I think about Chuck and Donald, and say a prayer for their families. I also know now that I was left here to share my story, to tell as many people as I can, and to give all the glory to God for what He has had in store for my life.

My support system started to take shape when I was flown to

Bethesda after the explosion. And through the years, it just keeps getting stronger and stronger. I talked about my wife and children, but another major player in my support system is the United Service Organizations (USO).

This was an event hosted by the USO and the White House, Summer 2009, after the Steelers won the Super Bowl that year. They visited the White House and we made USO care packages to send to troops overseas alongside the Steeler players.

For decades many comedians, musicians, actors, athletes, and celebrities from across the nation have been advocates for and spend time visiting with wounded warriors or deployed service members. I was so grateful to meet several of them during my time at Bethesda. There were so many different people that came into the hospital to lift our spirits and to let us know America was standing behind us.

My favorite famous visitor was P!NK. She's so great and so funny, and spent ten minutes talking with me (it doesn't seem like a lot of time, but there were a lot of wounded warriors she was seeing that day). She was in Washington D.C. for a concert and made the choice to visit us. P!NK's brother was in the USAF and her dad also served. She is just a total class act.

Another support process put into place for wounded warriors is Salute Military Golf Association (SMGA). I heard about them while at Bethesda and decided that I would give it a try. Golf had been one of the sports I wanted to learn anyway, so having this program nearby, in Olney, Maryland, made it the perfect time to take up the game. Jim Estes, a professional golfer in the 1980s, ran the program because of his desire to help veterans who had been injured in combat. I went to the clinic and began learning how to play. Later, in fall 2008, the Senior PGA Championship came to Baltimore, Maryland. They invited several groups of four veterans to come and play with a senior professional golfer. Because of being a part of SMGA, I was asked if I wanted to go. I did want to go but I didn't even own a set of clubs at this point. They set me up with a set of clubs, and although I wasn't anywhere near good enough to help our team come close to winning, I went and our group was partnered with Fuzzy Zeller. It was a blast and I am glad our group was with Fuzzy. He is such a great guy and extremely funny. He had us laughing from the time we met, on the course, and even afterwards. Fuzzy was so easy going that he would just jump right in and start cutting up with us and cracking jokes. It was a great time. I was scheduled for knee surgery the following week and this experience gave me a chance to forget about the seriousness of my injuries and laugh until my sides hurt.

I continued going to golf clinics In the spring of 2009 through SMGA and Disabled Sports USA, a program that helps disabled people whether you are military or civilian. Both of these groups are also affiliated with Ping, a company in Arizona that makes golf clubs. Together, these three groups provided us with an opportunity to get a set of Ping clubs for free if we attended six of the eight clinics. Ping even sent a representative to our club to fit us for our golf clubs. I only missed one clinic because I had been invited to go to the Monday after-the Masters event. It's an event put on by Hootie and the Blowfish in Myrtle Beach, South Carolina. My group went down for a weekend and played golf. On Monday, Hootie and the Blowfish invited a bunch of their friends to play with us in a tournament-style golf outing. Monday night, at the House of Blues in Myrtle Beach, Hootie and the Blowfish put on a concert for all of us. Darius Rucker did some of his solo work, too. Singer Josh Kelly, married to Katherine Heigl, Josh's brother, Charles Kelly, singer with Lady Antebellum, and their other brother, Michael, all performed. Michael is not really a professional singer but that man can sing some Led Zeppelin. Edwin McCain also performed. Other celebrities were in the audience with us, Samuel L. Jackson and Steve Spurrier, and they would just sit and talk with us as if they had known us all their lives. I returned from that weekend experience feeling quite proud of my military service and I received my free set of custom-fit Ping golf clubs.

The Semper Fi Fund (SFF) has also been a great support system. They have a team, called Team Semper Fi (TSF), which deals with recovery through sport. When I started getting into triathlons, they were right there to support me, sending me to triathlons across the country, paying for my coach and training programs, paying for my gear, and paying for my lodging in Florida for Ironman. They made sure that my mom had what she needed when traveling back and forth to Bethesda immediately after my accident. Semper Fi Fund also provides grants to injured service members or their family members in the event that someone is struggling with bills, or has specific needs due to their injuries. For example, they provide iPads to injured veterans who have suffered traumatic brain injuries so that they can keep their minds sharp and active using various brain games from the app store. My favorite event is their annual Marine Corps Marathon in Washington D.C. This is a family event and they allow you to bring your family members for the weekend. It's also a great time to reunite with the guys I have met since I have been involved with SFF and TSF. Both the volunteers and the other wounded veterans continue to inspire me year after year at MCM. The camaraderie we share is unlike anything I've ever experienced.

I am a Christian and I believe in the Father, Son, and Holy Ghost but I do not place myself on a pedestal. Each day, when I wake up and before I go to sleep, I am intentional about giving thanks to God. I need to remember that I have to give Him thanks and praise for my support system and for the ability to forgive.

When I started this journey of writing down my own story from tragedy to success, I knew that I would have to open up about some of the most painful experiences of my life. Sharing these wounds, both physical and emotional, is not intended to garner sympathy from anyone. My intent is to show you that I have put into action my Four Steps and wake up every day with a full heart. Notice I didn't say pain free, because there are days, sometimes weeks, where the pain is unbearable. When this happens, my wife and kids know exactly the

Family Portrait, 2017.

right things to do to make me laugh and get me out of my zone. I put my words into actions, and with a grateful heart, I have been able to keep the pain in perspective and find joy in each and every day. I promise you, you can find your own way, too.

ACKNOWLEDGMENTS AND INFLUENCES

The first person I can remember who made a positive impact on my life was Brian Mott from the trailer park I grew up in. Brian was an all-around great guy. It didn't matter that he was about 10 years or so older than I was, if he had time to play with me and the other kids, or let us hang out with him while he fed his snake, then he did. Having someone do that when you are so young is a huge benefit. I enjoyed all the time I got to spend with Brian and his pets, and when he joined the Air Force, I didn't get to see him as much. Unfortunately, there really weren't many other positive role models to look up to in the trailer park at that time.

My 5th grade teacher was very influential. She was always upbeat and had a smile on her face. I hardly remember her ever raising her voice or yelling. Her name then was Tammy Crone; I am not sure what her married name is today, but I know she got married and moved to New Jersey, at least that was the last I heard. Seeing her smile and having someone who was always so positive, is a great memory. She played a big role in teaching me to smile all the time.

My favorite teacher from middle school was Tina Doggett, she then got married and was Tina Martin, but I do not know where she is now nor do I have any contact with her. She was always positive and pushing me to be better and do better. I hated to read and do book reports in school, but she helped me to learn to like them more. I remember the first full chapter book I read was in her class in 7th or 8th grade, I just don't remember the name of the book. Having her to push me to be a better person, she definitely made an impact on me to be who I am today.

One of my best friends throughout middle and high school, who was like a sister to me was Kelly Backert, now Kelly Ellison. Kelly was always smiling and had a very upbeat personality. She loved Jesus and always let His light shine through her every day. Little did I know that a message she wrote in my middle school yearbook that simply said, "God loves you so much," would be a turning point for me, as I would read my yearbooks when I was bored. When I came across her message, I knew I wanted to start going to church, but I did not know how big of a role it would play in my life. After visiting Kelly's church for a few weeks, I decided to give my life to Christ and I haven't been the same since. Through meeting and knowing Kelly, her family became like my own family. I would go there and sit and visit with her and her parents whenever I wanted to and it was great. I had positive role models through them, and being with them was always nice. Sometimes I would go over just to visit, and other times I went so that I could ask questions that I had about God. Having them help me in my spiritual growth was vital to my early walk with Christ. Her parents, Jim and Marlene, and her older brother, Chris, were like my own spiritual family and I'm thankful to have had them in my life at just the right time.

I'll never forget my high school German teacher, Mr. Ulf Grabowski. He was an amputee; his right arm was amputated below his elbow, but he would show us that he could do ranger push-ups. This is where his feet were elevated on a table and he would do push-ups at an angle. That was very encouraging to me. I didn't realize it in high school, but he would have a huge impact in my recovery. You see, Mr. Grabowski did not let anything stop him from living the life he wanted to live. Seeing that throughout my high school career and interacting with him some after high school as well made a big impact on me. Seeing his attitude was probably one of the biggest things that allowed me to overcome my own injuries and the Ironman.

The next person I want to mention is a co-worker from my days at Colonial Honda. Jimmy Ludwigsen is a great father and raised his daughter Kelsi to be someone who has a lot of respect for her elders and someone who wants to change the world by helping people. Jimmy taught me a lot about what it's like to be a great father, while balancing work and life. As a mechanic, Jimmy would work long hours, and every other Saturday, but he still had a great family life. Greg Ewing, the other mechanic at Colonial Honda, was the same way. He would always make time for his family and I am still in touch with him, as he is still my mechanic. Both of his sons have turned out to be respectable young men. Seeing the way these two gentlemen interacted with their families has taught me a lot about having a great work/family balance.

Damian Goodman is one of my favorite Staff Sergeants that I ever served with. He came to Bravo Company, 1st Battalion 3rd Marines (1/3), when I was with them before I volunteered to go to Iraq with 2/3 and Echo Company. He took me under his wing when I was making poor choices in Hawaii. On the weekends, we would hang out, barbecue, and just relax. He eventually bought a motorcycle and we would ride together occasionally. I was headed to Iraq, so we didn't have a lot of time to ride together, but he was a great friend and leader.

Marcus Wilson was the platoon leader in Iraq, and one of the Marines who saved my life. He has become one of the people whose brain I can pick for everyday advice when I need it. Marcus is like a brother to me and the way he stepped up and stepped in to save me is remarkable. Without him, I would not be here today. He is someone who can make anyone laugh. The things he says and the way he tells me stories about what happened the day I was injured or what happened after I left Iraq before he was injured, is just funny to me and when we get together it is just a blast. He now lives in

California, so we don't get to see each other much, but when we do, we always have a good time.

James Steuter is the other Marine who saved my life, and is also like a brother. It is always good to catch up with him and see how his family is doing. Whenever we get the chance to talk on the phone or through text, we always make sure to check on each other and on our families. James is great guy to talk to, he lives in Colorado and I haven't seen him since the Memorial Service in Hawaii. We try to make plans to meet up if he is heading out to the East Coast to see some of his wife's family in the New England area, that way we can watch a Red Sox game together.

My triathlon coach, Billy Edwards, was a Naval Academy graduate. He was coaching the Naval Academy Triathlon team when I first reached out to ask him about coaching me. After hearing my story, he really wanted to work with me and he wanted me to be comfortable in my budget and what I was paying him each month. We worked together for the majority of my triathlon years and it was a great experience. With both of us being Veterans, we worked together well. He was a great motivator on rides and runs when we got together and met in Annapolis for training. He really helped me with my speed, nutrition, and saving my legs on the bike ride to be able to complete the run. He was also there when I did Ironman in Florida cheering me on, running around the course motivating me and helping me get through my run when all I wanted to do was walk. It was great having him there with me and beside me on the course, during moments I will never forget. Even though I am no longer doing triathlons, we still stay in touch and check in with one another every few months.

Every Chief, Senior Chief, and Master Chief I had in the Navy were all great leaders. Each one of them made sure that they looked out for their sailors first and that is important. There is a huge difference in my eyes between a leader and a supervisor and the military is really good about developing leaders. I believe the biggest reason this is true is because they were all in our shoes at one point, and they were out there in the field, getting dirty right beside us. When you get out into the civilian world and even the Federal Government, not all of the supervisors are great leaders. Some of them feel like they are entitled to be a supervisor because they have put in so many years of service and deserve their position, but they don't know how to lead people. They suck the life and morale right out of their people by constantly throwing work at you when there is not any help or enough people there in your department to get the work done. That is why I was grateful for so many awesome Chiefs who really showed me how to lead and how to put other people first. I would say that joining the Navy definitely helped me in serving others better.

Patricia O'Connor, my first supervisor in my first government job, was also a great leader. She worked her way up from an intern to a director and she really focused on taking care of her team. Her main goal was to make sure that everyone was given the opportunity to develop and advance in their career. She was always willing to listen and allow you to vent your personal problems to her, and she always offered great advice. I'm not sure I would have gotten through my separation and divorce without her guidance and encouragement. There were times we laughed together, cried together and were inspired by one another. I am forever grateful for the opportunity she gave me to join her team when I first became a government employee, and I will always remember the awesome leader she was.

The Brown family has had such a positive influence on my life. I am honored to know them, and to consider them family. To see their outlook on life after losing their youngest son, Donald, in the IED explosion I was involved in is remarkable. When I met them in Hawaii at the Memorial Service in April 2007, the first thing I did was apologize for not being able to save their son or do anything to try to help him. They gave me a hug and told me everything was okay and that it was God's will that Donald was no longer with us. That was a bit of a relief to me, but at the same time I was still dealing with survivor's guilt. Then we got in contact through Facebook and I went to visit them at their home in New Jersey a year or two later, when my oldest daughter was still a baby. I recently went to their family farm in New York for the 10 year anniversary of the accident and got to see the entire family again and spend time with them. This was a great blessing for me and they treated me like their own. I am so grateful for them and the love they've shown me since the accident. I can definitely see the love of Jesus shining through them and I cannot wait to visit with them again.

My wife Jennifer and my kids are my inspiration to live every day. When I get muscle spasms in my back and they continue to go on for a week straight, and the pain becomes unbearable, they are the reason I push through and continue to live my life. Believe me, there are times when the pain is so bad and I wish that God would have taken me out of this world in that accident, but I always remember that I am here to share this story and to show my kids what true love really is. I am constantly striving to serve my wife and love her as Christ loves His church and showing my kids what kind of sacrifice He made for us on the cross. I am so grateful that God allowed me to stay here on this earth to have kids and raise them to the best of my ability. I am thankful to be able to show them His love, to be able to act like a kid when I play with them, and to be able to be stern and discipline when they need it, because I love them enough to show them the right way and not allow them to live a life full of bad decisions.

Larry D. Perry III

Larry D. Perry III is a Purple Heart Recipient, Ironman Finisher and graduate of American Corporate Partner's (ACP) Mentorship program. He was born and raised in Small Town USA, but found himself calling several bigger cities home during his time in the Navy. As the sole survivor of an IED blast in Iraq in 2006, he learned to rely on his faith in God to overcome adversity during his recovery from thirty surgeries. Over the course of a few years, he realized he was using the same four steps to get through each trial. He now hopes to help others overcome their own trials and tribulations using the same technique.

Larry currently resides in Lancaster, PA with his wife and children, where they lead a healthy, active lifestyle. A Doc's Testimony: From Injury to Ironman is his first literary venture.

Made in the USA
San Bernardino, CA
21 November 2017